DOVER · THRIFT · EDITIONS

Great Speeches on Gay Rights

EDITED BY
JAMES DALEY

DOVER PUBLICATIONS, INC.
Mineola, New York

DOVER THRIFT EDITIONS
GENERAL EDITOR: MARY CAROLYN WALDREP
EDITOR OF THIS VOLUME: JANET BAINE KOPITO

Acknowledgements

August Bebels's "Address at the Reichstag" courtesy of John Lauritsen, copyright © 1978; Kurt Hiller's "A 1928 Gay Rights Speech" courtesy of John Lauritsen, published in John Lauritsen and David Thorstad's *The Early Homosexual Rights Movement: 1864–1935*, Times Change Press, Second Revised Edition, 1995.

Franklin Kameny's "Civil Liberties: A Progress Report" courtesy of Franklin Kameny.

Elizabeth Birch's "Text of First Convention Speech by a Gay Organization's Leader," Eric Rofes's "The Emerging Sex Panic Targeting Gay Men," Jack Nichols's "Why I Joined the Movement," and Jim Kepner's "Why Can't We All Get Together, and What Do We Have in Common?" all courtesy of GayToday.com

Harvey Milk's "The Hope Speech" courtesy of the San Francisco Public Library.

Sue Hyde's "We Gather in Dubuque" copyright © 1988 by Sue Hyde; courtesy of Sue Hyde.

Urvashi Vaid's "Speech at the March on Washington" courtesy of Urvashi Vaid.

Sally Gearhart's "The Lesbian and God-the-Father" courtesy of Sally Gearhart.

Anna Rueling's "What interest does the women's movement have in solving the homosexual problem?" courtesy of Michael Lombardi-Nash, who also did the translation.

Bibliographical Note

Great Speeches on Gay Rights is a new compilation, first published by Dover Publications, Inc., in 2010. James Daley has selected and arranged the speeches and provided all the introductory material. For the sake of authenticity, inconsistencies in spelling, capitalization, and punctuation have been retained in the texts.

Library of Congress Cataloging-in-Publication Data

Great speeches on gay rights / [edited by] James Daley.
  p. cm.
  ISBN-13: 978-0-486-47512-7
  ISBN-10: 0-486-47512-3
 1. Gay rights. 2. Speeches, addresses, etc. I. Daley, James, 1979–
HQ76.5.G74 2010
323.3'264—dc22

2010002341

Manufactured in the United States by Courier Corporation
47512302   2014
www.doverpublications.com

Introduction

THE HISTORY of America is the history of a hundred different marches seeking freedom from oppression. The Pilgrims' journey to escape religious persecution helped found a nation in which all people can worship freely in whatever manner they choose; in a country where only land-owning white men could vote, suffrage was revised to disregard race and gender; from a nation built on the backs of thousands of African slaves, America has grown into a country presided over by its first African-American president. This is the essential evolution of rights in America: over time, and often with great struggle and bloodshed, we shed our injustices, we expand our liberty, and we grow our freedom. Yet, as any same-sex couple who has been denied a marriage license for no reason other than their gender can state: our freedom still has a bit more growing to do.

The selection of speeches in this volume aims to give but a glimpse into the progress of freedom and equality for homosexuals and lesbians both in America and around the world. In August Bebel's 1898 "Address at the Reichstag" we encounter a German politician arguing (unsuccessfully, for the time being) for the repeal of an unenforceable law making homosexual behavior a crime. Later, in Anna Rueling's "What interest does the women's movement have in solving the homosexual problem?" we see the women's rights movement joining forces with the gay rights movement, as people finally began to realize that to have civil rights for anyone, we must have civil rights for everyone. Later still, we have the 1960s speeches of Jack Nichols and Franklin Kameny, both calling out for Americans to take advantage of the great strides being made in civil rights and extend these freedoms to all, regardless of sexual orientation. In 1978, Harvey Milk delivered his immortal "Hope Speech," as relevant today as it was at that crucial turning point in the history of the movement. The eighties and nineties provide a slew of speeches by brilliant orators, including Harry Hay, Sue Hyde, Urvashi Vaid, and Jim Kepner—all urging an end to the anti-gay laws and the homophobia that have plagued our nation for so long.

Finally, we have the speeches of Evan Wolfson, Paul Martin, and Ian Hunter, arguing the single issue that has thus far defined the gay rights movement in the twenty-first century: the desire for marriage equality. In the midst of this struggle, it is easy to get lost in politics and rhetoric and lose sight of just how personal an issue it is. That's why the Australian legislator Ian Hunter's speech may be the most poignant in this anthology. Hunter, addressing anti-gay marriage Prime Minister Kevin Rudd directly, says:

I am no longer content to accept the crumbs from the table.

I am no longer willing to accept a reinforced second-class status.

I am no longer prepared to accept a proposition that my married friends' relationships are intrinsically superior to my relationship.

And I certainly won't accept the proposal that means my relationship is registered at the local council or some similar body.

Because partnership registration is about *death*—and what happens to your estate on your death. Marriage is about *life*—how you live your life publicly in a loving relationship with a partner and with our *families*. . . .

Because I want to get married—and you, Mr. Rudd, are stopping me.

And that, perhaps, is how this freedom, too, may finally be won: by getting people at all levels of society—citizens and politicians, activists and clergy—to understand that this is fundamentally just another story of one man pursuing his own happiness, and another man endeavoring to stop him. And that is not freedom.

James Daley
Editor

Contents

Great Speeches on Gay Rights

Robert G. Ingersoll

Address at the Funeral of Walt Whitman
(Camden, New Jersey, March 30, 1892)

Robert Green Ingersoll [1833–1899] was a noted agnostic, a political leader in the Republican Party, one of the most highly acclaimed orators of the nineteenth century, and a close friend of Walt Whitman. He gave this speech before a crowd of several thousand at Whitman's funeral services at the Harleigh Cemetery in Camden, New Jersey.

AGAIN, WE, in the mystery of Life, are brought face to face with the mystery of Death. A great man, a great American, the most eminent citizen of this Republic, lies dead before us, and we have met to pay tribute to his greatness and his worth.

I know he needs no words of mine. His fame is secure. He laid the foundations of it deep in the human heart and brain. He was, above all I have known, the poet of humanity, of sympathy. He was so great that he rose above the greatest that he met without arrogance, and so great that he stooped to the lowest without conscious condescension. He never claimed to be lower or greater than any of the sons of men.

He came into our generation a free, untrammeled spirit, with sympathy for all. His arm was beneath the form of the sick. He sympathized with the imprisoned and despised, and even on the brow of crime he was great enough to place the kiss of human sympathy.

One of the greatest lines in our literature is his, and the line is great enough to do honor to the greatest genius that has ever lived. He said, speaking of an outcast, "Not until the sun excludes you will I exclude you."

His charity was as wide as the sky, and wherever there was human suffering, human misfortune, the sympathy of Walt bent above it as the firmament bends above the earth.

He was built on a broad and splendid plan—ample, without appearing to have limitations—passing easily for a brother of mountains and seas and constellations; caring nothing for the little maps and charts with which timid pilots hug the shore, but giving himself freely with the recklessness of genius to winds and waves and tides; caring for nothing so long as the stars were above him. He walked among men, among writers, among verbal varnishers and veneerers, among literary milliners and tailors, with the unconscious majesty of an antique god.

He was the poet of that divine democracy which gives equal rights to all the sons and daughters of men. He uttered the great American voice; uttered a song worthy of the great Republic. No man has ever said more for the rights of humanity, more in favor of real democracy, of real justice. He neither scorned nor cringed; was neither tyrant nor slave. He asked only to stand the equal of his fellows beneath the great flag of nature, the blue and the stars.

He was the poet of life. It was a joy simply to breathe. He loved the clouds; he enjoyed the breath of morning, the twilight, the winds, the winding streams. He loved to look at the sea when the waves burst into the whitecaps of joy. He loved the fields, the hills; he was acquainted with the trees, with birds, with all the beautiful objects of the earth. He not only saw these objects, but understood their meaning, and he used them that he might exhibit his heart to his fellow men.

He was the poet of Love. He was not ashamed of that divine passion that has built every home; that divine passion that has painted every picture and given us every real work of art; that divine passion that has made the world worth living in and has given some value to human life.

He was the poet of the natural, and taught men not to be ashamed of that which is natural. He was not only the poet of democracy, not only the poet of the great Republic, but he was the poet of the human race. He was not confined to the limits of this country, but his sympathy went out over the seas to all the nations of the earth.

He stretched out his hands and felt himself the equal of all kings and of all princes, and the brother of all men, no matter how high, no matter how low.

He has uttered more supreme words than any writer of our century, possibly of almost any other. He was, above all things, a man, and above genius, above all the snow-capped peaks of intelligence, above all art, rises the true man.

He was the poet of Death. He accepted all life and all death, and he justified all. He had the courage to meet all, and was great enough and splendid enough to harmonize all and to accept all there is as divine melody.

You know better than I what his life has been, but let me say one thing: Knowing as he did, what others can know and what can not, he accepted and absorbed all theories, all creeds, all religions, and believed in none. His philosophy was a sky that embraced all clouds and accounted for all clouds. He had a philosophy and a religion of his own, broader, as he believed—and as I believe—than others. He accepted all, he understood all, and he was above all.

He was absolutely true to himself. He had frankness and courage, and he was as candid as light. He was willing that all the sons of man should be absolutely acquainted with his heart and brain. He had nothing to conceal. Frank, candid, pure, serene, noble, and yet for years he was maligned and slandered simply because he had the candor of nature. He will be understood yet, and that for which he was condemned his frankness, his candor—will add to the glory and greatness of his fame.

He wrote a liturgy for mankind; he wrote a great and splendid psalm of life, and gave to us the gospel of humanity—the greatest gospel that can be preached.

He was not afraid to live; not afraid to die. For many years he and Death lived near neighbors. He was always willing and ready to meet and greet this king called Death, and for many months he sat in the deepening twilight waiting for the night, waiting for the light.

He never lost his hope. When the mists filled the valleys, he looked upon the mountain tops, and when the mountains in darkness disappeared, fixed his gaze upon the stars.

In his brain were the blessed memories of the day and in his heart were mingled the dawn and dusk of life.

He was not afraid; he was cheerful every moment. The laughing nymphs of day did not desert him. They remained that they might clasp the hands and greet with smiles the veiled and silent sisters of the night. And when they did come, Walt Whitman stretched his hand to them. On one side were the nymphs of day, and on the other the silent sisters of the night, and so, hand in hand, between smiles and tears, he reached his journey's end.

From the frontier of life, from the western wave-kissed shore, he sent us messages of content and hope, and these messages seem now like strains of music blown by the "Mystic Trumpeter" from Death's pale realm.

Today we give back to Mother Nature, to her clasp and kiss, one of the bravest, sweetest souls that ever lived in human clay.

Charitable as the air and generous as Nature, he was negligent of all except to do and say what he believed he should do and say.

And today I thank him, not only for you but for myself, and for all the brave words he has uttered. I thank him for all the great and splendid words he has said in favor of liberty, in favor of man and woman, in favor of motherhood, in favor of fathers, and I thank him for the brave words he has said of death.

He has lived, he has died, and death is less terrible than it was before. Thousands and millions will walk down in to the "dark valley of the shadow" holding Walt Whitman by the hand. Long after we are dead the brave words he has spoken will sound like trumpets to the dying.

And so I lay this little wreath upon this great man's tomb. I loved him living, and I love him still.

August Bebel

Address at the Reichstag
(Berlin, Germany, January 13, 1898;
translated by John Lauritsen)

August Ferdinand Bebel [1840–1913] was best known as an outspoken member of the German parliament (Reichstag) in the late nineteenth century, where he was one of the founders of the Social Democratic Party. In this speech, Bebel argues in favor of repealing Paragraph 175 of the German penal code—the law that criminalized homosexuality. It is widely believed to be the first political speech in favor of homosexual freedoms.

REPRESENTATIVES: UNDERSTANDABLE is the position of those who, deeply offended by certain distasteful aspects of our public and private life, endeavor to make the fullest use of the criminal code to remedy these evils and wipe them off the face of the earth. My friends and I are also prepared to second a large number of the provisions which Dr. Spahn and his colleagues have proposed in the draft before us, but by no means all. On the one hand, this draft goes too far from our standpoint, and on the other, not far enough. In particular, once reform has been accomplished in this area, we should have to consider whether there may not be still other comparable provisions of our penal code that have at least as much right and as much need to be revised as the paragraphs here proposed.

5

Gentlemen, the penal code exists to be enforced—that is to say, so that the authorities who have the primary responsibility for maintaining compliance with and respect for the law should be dutifully watchful for violations and act accordingly. But there are provisions of our penal code, some of them contained in the motion before us, where the authorities, although fully aware that these provisions are systematically violated by a great number of people, men as well as women, only in the rarest cases bother to call for action on the part of the prosecutor. Here I have particularly in mind the section with the provisions of Paragraph 175—it has to do with "unnatural fornication." It will be necessary, if the Commission is elected—and I do urge that one be, because in my opinion this bill cannot become law without the Commission's recommendation—that then the government of Prussia be specifically requested to remand to us certain material which the local Berlin vice squad has at its disposal, so that on the basis of an examination of the same, we may ask ourselves whether we can and should retain the section with the provisions of Paragraph 175, and, if we should, whether we should not have to expand them. I am informed by the best sources that the police of that city do not bring the names of men who commit offenses which Paragraph 175 makes punishable by imprisonment to the attention of the district attorney as soon as they have become aware of the fact, but rather add the names of the persons involved to the list of those who for the same reasons are already in their files.

(Hear! Hear! [from the Left])

The number of these persons is so great and reaches so far into all levels of society, that if the police here scrupulously carried out their duty, the Prussian State would immediately be compelled to build two new penitentiaries just to take care of those offenses against Paragraph 175 that are committed in Berlin alone.

(Commotion. Hear! Hear!)

That is not an exaggeration, Herr von Levetzow; it has to do with thousands of persons from all walks of life. But then it further raises the question of whether the provisions of Paragraph 175 should apply not only to men, but also to women who on their part commit the same offense. What is just in the case of one sex, is fair for the other. But gentlemen, I'll tell you this: if in this area the Berlin police did their duty all the way—I want to say a word about this—then there would be a scandal such as the world have never known, a scandal compared with which the Panama scandal, the Dreyfus scandal, the Lützow-Ledert and the Tausch-Normann scandals are pure child's play. Perhaps this is one of the reasons why the offense punishable under this Paragraph is treated with such extraordinary laxity on the part of the police. Gentlemen, Paragraph 175 is part of the penal code, and because it is there, it must be enforced. However, if for whatever reasons this part of the criminal law cannot be enforced, or can be enforced only selectively, then the question arises whether this provision of the penal code can equitably be retained. I wish to venture that in this very session—perhaps some of the gentlemen may not yet have taken note of it—we have before us a printed petition signed by me personally, among others, and by a number of colleagues from other parties, and further by people from literary and academic circles, by jurists of the most illustrious standing, by psychologists and pathologists, by experts of the highest rank in this field. The petition, for reasons that understandably I don't wish to go into fully at this moment, advocated a revision of the penal code so as to repeal the relevant provisions of Paragraph 175.

The translator, John Lauritsen, has been a gay activist and writer since 1969. His Gay Liberation pages can be viewed at http://paganpressbooks .com/GAYLIB.HTM

Anna Rueling

*What interest does the women's movement have
in solving the homosexual problem?*
(Berlin, Germany, October 8, 1904)

*Dr. Anna Rueling [1880–1953] was a prominent German physician in
the early twentieth century, and is widely considered to be the first lesbian
activist. In this speech, delivered at Berlin's Prinz Albrecht Hotel, Rueling argues that the struggle for women's rights is one and the same with
the struggle for homosexual freedoms.*

LADIES AND Gentlemen,

The Women's Movement is an historico-cultural necessity.

Homosexuality is an historico-cultural necessity, and is an
obvious and natural bridge between man and woman. Today
this is an undisputed scientific fact about which ignorance and
impatience cannot dispute. Many have asked how I came to this
conclusion and have uttered the truth about historico-cultural and
natural-historical concepts in the same breath, two things which
on the surface seem to be opposite.

The interest to research the reason for this extended viewpoint
is that one in general, when the matter concerns homosexuals,
thinks only of male Urnings and overlooks how many female
homosexuals there are. They are of course less discussed because
they—I was just about to say "unfortunately"—have had no

8

unjust cause to fight against such as penal code paragraphs which arise out of having false moral views.

No cruel justice menaces women nor does the penitentiary if they follow their natural instincts. But the mental pressure under which Urninds are is just as great, indeed even greater than the yoke which their male fellow-sufferers must bear. To the world which judges by outward appearances they are even more obvious than the female Urning. Only too often they are overwhelmed by people's moralized misunderstandings.

In our total social life, however, Uranian women are at least just as important as their male counterparts because they influence our lives in many ways, even if they are not discussed. If one would just observe, one would soon come to the conclusion that homosexuality and the Women's Movement do not stand opposed to each other, but rather they aid each other reciprocally to gain rights and recognition, and to eliminate the injustice which condemns them on this earth.

The Homosexual Movement fights for the rights of all homosexuals, for men as for women. The Scientific Humanitarian Committee has distinguished itself by taking interest in this fight to the advantage of all other movements which should have, and has also participated in the interest of Urninds with such lively dedication.

The Women's Movement strives to have its long-despised rights recognized. It fights, namely, for as much independence as possible and for a just and equal standing of women with men, married or unmarried. These latter strivings are especially important because firstly, of the condition of our present economical state, and secondly, because a great number of women will remain unmarried due to a statistical nominal surplus of women in the population of our fatherland. These women are forced, when a sufficient means of earning money is not at their disposal away from the home—which is only the case of approximately 10%—to take up the fight for life and win their bread by any means available.

The homosexual women's position and participation in the Women's Movement in its all-important problem is of the greatest and the most decisive importance and deserves the most basic and extensive analysis.

One must differentiate between the homosexual woman's personality as well as her sexual instinct. Most important, of course, is her personality in general. In the second place is the tendency of her sexual drive, which, without the exact knowledge of her tendency, no unbiased evaluation could be rendered, because of the incapability to make full and just considerations of the same, because the physical sex drive is almost always just an overflow, naturally following psychical characteristics; i.e., in persons with dominant masculine characteristics it is directed toward women and vice versa, always without taking into account the outer bodily structure.

Homosexual women have many characteristics, inclinations and abilities which we usually consider as valid for men. They take a much less interest in the emotional life than the average woman. While for the expressly heterosexual woman, feeling is almost always—even here exceptions prove the rule—dominant and decisive, while mostly a sharp clarity and reason predominate in the Urnind. She is, as in the average, normal man, more objective, more energetic and goal oriented than the feminine woman; she thinks and feels like a man; she does not imitate men; she is conditioned as he; this is the all-decisive point which haters and calumniators of so-called "men-women" always ignore, because they do not even take the time to do basic research on the homosexual. It is easy to judge what one does not understand, and it is just as easy, as it would only seem to be difficult to correct a pre-established and false opinion, to correct them by reasoning. I would like to note that there is an absolute and a separate psychic homosexuality, that, therefore, masculine characteristics do not necessarily and unconditionally result in the sexual drive being forced towards one's own sex; because each Urnind naturally possesses numerous feminine characteristics to a certain degree, which may be expressed in one of the numerous intermediate stages in the transitional stages between the sexes, even by being sexually attracted to a man.

Of course, the drive in these cases is in most cases directed to a very effeminate man, as a natural completion of the woman who has a strong masculine soul.

I recall, for example, George Sand and Daniel Stern, who both loved men, those of the side of the feminine, Friedrich Chopin and Franz Liszt. Clara Schumann, the great artist, also, was married to a man who had strong feminine characteristics—Robert Schumann. It seems, moreover, as if in the women I have characterized as psychic homosexuals, the sex drive was never especially strongly developed; even George Sand and Daniel loved their artists much more with their souls than with their senses; therefore, I am inclined to speak of psychic homogenic women somewhat as "sexless" natures.

Since a woman who has a masculine nature and masculine traits would never satisfactorily fulfill a full-fledged man, without further ado, it is clear that the Urnind is not suitable for marriage. Even Uranian women know this is true or feel this way. Unconsciously and naturally they voluntarily refuse to walk up the aisle to the justice of the peace.

But how often had they to deal with parents, cousins, aunts, and other dear friends and relatives who, day in and day out, tried to talk them into the necessity of marriage and make life a misery with their wise advice. Often, as young girls, they had to blindly fall into marriage, and thanks to our stunted education, without having a clear view and understanding of sexuality and sexual life.

As long as it remains the opinion of so-called society that late spinsterhood, namely, unmarried women, experience unpleasantness, indeed, that it is something demeaning, then it will occur only too often that the Urnind will allow herself to be driven to marry by exterior conditions, where she will find no happiness and be incapable of creating happiness. Such a marriage is far more immoral than the love which ties two persons when a powerful nature attracts them forcefully together.

The Women's Movement wants to reform marriage. It wishes to change many rights so that the inconsolable conditions of the present cease, so that discontent and injustice, arbitrary and slavish subjugation disappear out of the home of the family, so that a healthier and powerful race blossoms.

While striving for these reforms, the Women's Movement should not forget the amount of guilt it bears in the false, unfriendly evaluation of homosexual women. I say expressly, "how much guilt." Obviously far from it that I would want to burden the Women's Movement with full responsibility for this false evaluation. But for the sake of this portion of the guilt it is a simple and inescapable duty of the Women's Movement to explain to as many persons as possible by speaking and by writing how very destructive it is for homosexuals to enter into marriage.

First of all, naturally, for both partners' sake, the man is simply duped, because aside from its ideal meaning, entering into marriage is a two-sided contract in which both partners undertake duties and assume rights. A homosexual woman, however, can only fulfill her duties to the man with disinclination, in the best case, with indifference. A forced sexual communion is, without a doubt, a misery, and no conventional man could see anything to strive for or find happiness with a Uranian woman whom he wanted to marry.

It happens very often, that such a man will avoid sexual intercourse with her out of friendly sympathy and searches for sexual satisfaction of his drives in the arms of a mistress or with a prostitute. True morality and the health of our people concern the Women's Movement, which must do everything in its power to prevent homosexual marriages. And the Women's Movement can do much in the work of explaining to all circles that the marriage of Urninds creates a three-fold injustice: to the state, society and an unborn race. Because experience teaches that the successors of Uranian persons are only seldom healthy.

The unfortunate, unloved creatures are received unwanted and make up a great percentage of the number of weak-minded, idiotic, epileptic, chest-diseased degenerates of all sorts. Even unhealthy sexual drives such as sadism and masochism are often inherited by Uranian persons who have children against their nature. State and society should show an urgent interest to prevent Uranians from marrying, because later they must bear not such small portion of the care for such unhealthy and weak beings, from whom they may hardly expect a profit. A substantially more practical point for heterosexual women, it seems to me, is that if Urninds could remain unmarried without ruining [their] social reputation, they would find it much easier, as is their nature, to find the great satisfaction they do in the circle of the wife, housekeeper, and mother.

Still lacking, unfortunately, is an exact statistical survey of the number of homosexual women, but, taking into consideration my immense experience and thorough studies in this field, the result yielded by the statistical survey by Dr. Hirschfeld on the extensiveness of male homosexuality may also be applied to women.

According to this survey, there are as many Urninds as there are unmarried women. This should not be misunderstood. For example, I mean that there may be as many as two million unmarried women. Among the two million unmarried women there is a greater percentage of Urninds, let's say 50%, thus one million; among the homosexuals, however, there are again as many, approximately 50% who, because of external circumstances, are married, therefore, you may calculate that 50% of normal unmarried women have lost the opportunity to marry. The consequences are easy to deduce according to these figures. When Urninds are free of having to marry, the possibility of marriages for the heterosexual women would increase enormously.

But I do not mean to say that I present here a universal means to prevent late spinsterhood, because increasing animosity from men toward marriage has its roots more in social relationships. But this is not the place to speak about that. If, however, the Women's Movement forcefully takes the side of the homosexual in the marriage question, then it takes a step forward toward reaching beautiful and lofty goals, the original idea of marriage, and the love ties between men and women would then be allowed to attain their rightful place. It is an ethical requirement in order to daily smash the face of public contempt, which causes numerous marriages of circumstance, so that persons may enter into marriage because they love one another.

I noticed that many homosexual women marry because they become aware of their nature too late and thus become unhappy in their innocence and make themselves unhappy. Here, too, the Women's Movement may take a stand by speaking about the question of their education as youths—which they often do—also by demonstrating how important it is for those parents who notice the homosexual bent in older children and youths, to make a long, loving and exact observation—and honest and understanding observers can recognize it in many ways—to explain in an understandable way the essence of homosexuality and their own natural inclinations.

Doing this prevents early misery enormously, instead, as often happens, of trying by all kinds of means to force homosexual children to take the heterosexual path. One need not fear that effeminate heterosexual children may be considered homosexual and thus be made into homosexuals, because, in the first place, such a diagnosis would naturally have to come from an experienced medical doctor, and secondly, as experience has taught, neither education nor any such a thing can change the heterosexual drive into a homosexual one and vice versa.

Of course, a heterosexual person can be seduced into homosexual behavior, but this occurs out of curiosity, search for pleasure or as a surrogate for the absence of normal intercourse—the latter occurs in the case of the navy—but the innate drive is not changed because of this, because under normal circumstances this does not occur.

At this time I would like to repeat what Dr. Hirschfeld has often explained, that homosexuality is not class specific, that it occurs among the upper class no less than among the lower or vice versa. No father and no mother, neither of them, ladies and gentlemen, can know without a doubt if there is an Uranian child among their offspring.

In middle-class circles they believe, oddly enough, that among them homosexuality has no place, and from these circles the most annoying enemies recruit each other against the movement to free Uranian people. I would like to give as an example, that my father, when by chance he came to speak about homosexuality, explained with conviction, "nothing of the sort can happen in my family." The facts prove the opposite. I need add nothing to that statement.

To return to the question of marriage, I would like to make note that a homosexual woman never becomes what one refers to with the expression "old spinster." The situation is worth investigating because it easily makes the Urninds especially recognizable at a later age.

Just take a look at an unmarried woman between the ages of 30 and 50 years. You will notice none of the joked-about characteristics of the average unmarried, heterosexual woman. This observation is instructive. It proves that a reasonable and moderate gratification of the sexual drive keeps a woman happy, fresh, and active, while absolute abstinence easily develops those characteristics which we feel unpleasant in old spinsters, for example, unfriendliness, hysteria, etc.

In order to create the possibility for homosexuals and all women in general to be able to live according to their own nature, it is necessary to actively join the strivings of the movement, which wishes to open immense possibilities of education and new occupations.

Now I am touching a sore spot in the evaluation of the sexes. I believe that all people, in all good will, would agree, if we research again here what intention nature, which is never wrong, had when it created man, woman and the transitional stages between the two. And one would have to agree that it is wrong to place one sex higher than the other, as it were, to speak of a first class—the man—a second class—the woman—and a third class sex—the Uranians.

The sexes are not to be evaluated differently, because they are distinct. The facts which show clearly and naturally that men, women and Urnings are not qualified for all occupations cannot be altered by the Women's Movement—and it does not wish to. A feminine woman is already organically by nature determined above all to become a wife and mother. And she has the right to be proud of her natural destination, because an occupation more highly esteemed than motherhood does not exist.

The woman, wife and mother or who is one of both, should not forget the rest of the world—she should take part all the more in all events of public life—that she may be capable is the goal of the Women's Movement, and that is, indeed, one of its finest goals.

To the normal, I mean, to the totally masculine man, other functions are given by nature and are shown other ways, than to a woman. He is—it cannot be denied—predestined for the most part to undertake a rougher battle than the woman, and so, occupations are open to him which obviously remain closed to women, for example, the military, all occupations which demand heavy labor, etc. Obviously there is also a bridge upon which some occupations rest, ones which both men and women are able to equally fill according to each person's abilities.

The logic of enemies to the Women's Movement falls apart because it equates all women under the label "woman" without considering that nature never created two persons alike, that the opinion whether an occupation be for a man or a woman is solely a matter of inner, masculine or feminine character.

From this we may differentiate between a feminine individuality in which feminine characteristics dominate, a masculine one dominated by masculine characteristics, and finally a masculine-feminine or feminine-masculine individuality in which there is an equal mixture of both.

Because nature created different kinds of sexes does not mean to say that there is only one sphere of activity for women—the home—and for the man another—the world—rather, nature's intention was and is without a doubt that each person has the opportunity to reach the goal which one is able to fulfill by one's own means and merits.

The interrelationships of masculine and feminine characteristics in people is so endless that common sense tells us that each child—whether it is male or female is all the same—must reach independence. The adult will have to decide for itself whether its natural drives lead to home, world, marriage or unmarried life. There must be a freedom of the play of the energies, then one can make the best and surest decision between becoming one of the women who can and wants to take up an artistic or academic occupation outside the home, or one of those women who does not feel enough energy to do this. And again it is the responsibility of the parents, who should feel this as their holiest duty, to be just toward each child's individuality and to avoid a make-believe system of education to fit all circumstances.

Schools are another story which, naturally, cannot do without certain methods, but it must be agreed upon, when it concerns girls and boys, to get rid of the old madness that the brains of girls have a weaker aptitude than boys' brains. One need not fear that competition in all the occupations will get out of hand because of the possibilities of co-education—especially, as the enemies' side believes, in academic occupations. It is for these scientific occupations which homosexual women are best suited, because they have the ability of a greater objectivity, energy, and endurance which is often lacking in very feminine women.

These facts do not exclude the very capable heterosexual women doctors, jurists, etc., but in spite of this, I feel that, with her own interest in mind, the heterosexual woman will always find happiness in the most favorable way or find it more meaningful to marry and make herself a partner to a man who feels the same way about her, who not only loves her sexually but also esteems her as his equal mentally and who recognizes that his rights are, of course, just as valid as hers.

Men, women and homosexuals, thus would have equal opportunity in a goal-oriented education, and a broader range of opportunities in education would open to male and female youths. Men would become the bread-winners of a thinking and understanding partner, women would slowly reach a worthy and just and respected position, and the Urninds would be able to devote themselves freely to the occupation of their choice.

Just as a man oftentimes prefers to take up an occupation which is typical of a woman's occupation—for example, women's designing, nursing, the occupation of the cook, the servant—there are also occupations which Uranian woman are especially attracted to. As a matter of fact, a great number of homosexual women show up in the fields of medicine, law, and business and even in the creative arts. There are men who, like Weininger, believe that all great historical literary, scientific or otherwise known, important or famous women have been homosexuals.

According to my past statements, I do not have to especially accentuate that this highly one-sided view is unproved, because not only history, but also our own eyes daily show us the weakness in this theory. On the other hand, I would not deny that many important women have been homosexual, just to mention Sappho, Christine of Sweden, Sonja Kowlewska, Rosa Bonheur. However, it would seem strange if one wanted to classify Elizabeth of England and Catherine the Great of Russia as Uranian persons; the latter was perhaps bisexual—her many male and female "friendships" seem to imply this—a pure homosexual, however, she was not.

In opposition to the anti-feminists who claim that the female sex is inferior and who acknowledge only those women who exhibit strong masculine characteristics, I accept both as equals, but I am convinced that a homosexual woman is especially best suited to play a leading role in the enormous movement for the rights of women which is worldwide. And, in fact, from the very beginning of the Women's Movement to the present day it has been more often than not homogenic women who took over the leadership in numerous battles, who only by means of their energy does the average woman, indifferent to her nature and easily subjugating herself, be brought to the awareness of her worth as a person and of her inalienable rights.

I cannot and will not name anyone, because as long as homosexuality remains something criminal and is considered to be against nature, as in many circles, as something unhealthy, some women may be offended whom I would like to indicate as being homosexual. We must always be proper and dutiful and not be indiscreet, and the noble feelings of the Uranian love of a female

Women's-Rights-Fighter, as heterosexual sentimentality, do not belong before a public forum. One who has only just superficially followed the development of the Women's Movement, one who is acquainted with a few or many leading women, one who has a spark of understanding for homosexuals would soon pick out those female Women's-Rights-Fighters and would recognize that not the worst is among them.

If we weigh all the contributions which homosexual women make to the Women's Movement, one would be astounded that its large and influential organizations have not lifted a finger to obtain justice in the state and in society for the not so small number of its Uranian members, and that they have done absolutely nothing to this very day to protect so many of its most well-known and most worthy female predecessors in this battle from ridicule and scorn when they explain to the greater public about the true essence of Uranism.

One should never have found it so difficult to point out how the characteristics of the homosexual tendency express themselves more involuntarily and without the slightest personal, intentional assistance of appearance, speech, behavior, gesture, clothing, etc. And the Urninds concerned are most unjustly given up to the ridicule of unknowing persons. Also, notice that many homosexual women naturally do not always appear masculine, which would be in harmony with her nature. There are also numerous Urninds who appear completely feminine, who go through all the motions to hide their homosexuality, a comedy which makes them uncomfortable and under which they suffer.

I am well acquainted with the reason why this doubly exceptional hesitation exists, because the Women's Movement has handled even general sexual matters with an odd frankness and matter-of-factness. It is the fear that the movement would suffer because of the broach of the homosexual question by becoming active by flashing the human rights of homosexuals in the blind eyes of the ignorant masses. I cannot deny that having this fear so early in the movement is justified, and it should be avoided in order not to lose friends again, and there should be a fully unconditional apology made for the total ignorance of the homosexual problem in earlier times.

Today, however, when the movement is moving incessantly forward, when no bureaucratic wisdom, no bourgeois ignorance can be victorious over it any longer, today I must point out that a total rejection of the doubtless very important question is unjust, is an injustice which is brought upon the Women's Movement by itself in many cases.

The so-called "moderate" tendency will not help homosexuals one bit for the simple reason that deeds of this kind have no tendency at all. Victory will come as a sign of radicalism, and we expect that the radicals will change the direction and for once make it honestly and openly recognized; indeed, there is a great number of Urninds among us, and we owe them a word of thanks for their efforts and their work and for many a fine success.

I do not mean to say that all questions of the Women's Movement will be handled from the homosexual viewpoint, just as I do not ascribe all this success to the Urninds or even a greater portion of it—that would be just as insane as it is wrong to take no notice at all of the homosexual problem. The Women's Movement doubtless has greater and more important concerns than the freedom of homosexuals—but only by taking care of the lesser matters can these greater efforts be accomplished.

Therefore, the Women's Movement should not ascribe to the homosexual problem such a great importance; it does not need to go out into the streets to preach against the injustice of Uranians—it should not do this, because it would surely hurt our cause—I do not underestimate this at all; it needs only to act by giving due consideration to the homosexual question when it discusses sexual, ethical, economic, and general human relationships between the sexes. This it surely can do; and by doing this it will slowly carry out its educational goal without much ado.

Now I am coming to a point which in recent years has especially come into the sphere of our work in the Women's Movement—I am going to speak of prostitution. One may wish to speak of this from an ethical standpoint. No matter, one will have to deal with it now as in the past and as in the future. Personally, I consider prostitution to be a pitiful but necessary evil, which we will be able to put a halt to in more favorable times—a goal which is worth the effort in the long run.

The importance of the battle of the Women's Movement against the increase of prostitution and against genocidal venereal disease, it seems to me, is that approximately 20% of prostitutes are evidently homosexual. At first you may find it unusual that homosexuality and enduring sexual intercourse with men appear as the most paradoxical thing that could ever exist. To my question how it is possible that an Urnind becomes a prostitute, a "woman of the street" once answered that she views her sad task as a business—her sexual drive does not come under consideration at all. She satisfies this with her lover.

These women have conducted some foul business in the streets. When the Women's Movement has succeeded in opening all suitable occupations for women, carrying through an equal respect of the abilities and inclinations of each person, then there will no longer be any homosexual young women among prostitutes, and a great number of the heterosexual women will be able to nourish themselves better and with more humanity than by the bad social conditions of prostitution today. They would be able to immediately take up an occupation, because women would be taught understanding and independence in their youth.

A young woman who is hardened early for the struggle to make a living will end up on the streets less often than a young woman who lives without a knowledge of the most basic and natural facts of life. In a certain sense the battle of the homogenic woman for her social recognition is also a battle against prostitution, and again I stress, that in this struggle it is only a matter of restraining it and never of suppressing it fully.

One must not forget that when a more correct judgment of Uranism is reached in general, a great number of homosexual men who now, out of fear of being discovered go to a prostitute, which is very much against their nature, may abstain from them. This would naturally decrease the amount of venereal disease, although it would not cause a great decrease. But I believe it would be a worthwhile cause, because each individual case of syphilis or some other venereal disease which would be prevented means a contribution to the health of the people and thus one to the next generation, which is in the long run a gain for the fatherland.

The Women's Movement is fighting for the rights of free individuals and of self-determination. Therefore, it must recognize the despised spell which society casts on Uranians even today, which oppresses their rights and their duty to take a stand and fight the battle on the side of the Uranians as they do unwed mothers, women workers and many others who need it, and to fight for their rights and for their freedom in their battle against old-fashioned false opinions of morality, but when it is really immoral to render a morality which is the worst immorality when women have inalienable rights torn from them and when they now must struggle in bloody battle to recover them; when Uranians have inalienable human rights to their kind of love torn from them, a love which is just as pure and noble as heterosexual love when they are good people who so love. There are as many good people among homosexuals as among so-called "normal" people.

Most of all, I would like to avoid the appearance of estimating homosexuals too highly. I can assure you, ladies and gentlemen, I will not do that—I am well aware of the problems of homosexuality, but I also recognize its good side. Therefore, I would like to say that Uranians are no better or no worse than heterosexuals—they should not be treated differently, but only in a different way.

To conclude my statements I would like to emphasize again that homosexual women have done their part in the greater Women's Movement, that they are mostly responsible for activating the movement. They have suffered because of their masculine inclinations and natural characteristics, and because of the many, many injustices and hardships caused by laws, society, and the old morality which concerns women. Without the power and cooperation of the Urninds, the Women's Movement would not be so successful today, which it certainly is—which could easily be proven.

The Women's Movement and the movement for homosexual rights have thus far traveled on a dark road which has posted many obstacles in their way. Now it will become brighter and brighter around us and in the hearts of the people. This is not to say that the work of securing the rights of women and of Uranians has come to an end; we are still in the middle of two opposing sides, and many a bloody battle will have to be fought. There will be many victims of the injustice of laws which will deal the death-blow before both movements have reached their goal—to gain the freedom of each person.

Our ultimate goal will be reached when both movements recognize that they have many common interests for which to fight when it becomes necessary. And when, at times, as they will, hard times come to either side—that will not be the time for hesitation to stand up in defense against injustice and to march on to the victory which will surely be ours.

Revelation and truth are like the rising sun in the East—no power can force it out of its orbit. Slowly but surely it rises to its glittering zenith! Perhaps not today or tomorrow, but in the not too distant future the Women's Movement and Uranians will raise their banners in victory!

Per aspera ad astra! (Reach for the stars!)

Kurt Hiller

*Appeal to the Second International Congress
for Sexual Reform on Behalf of
an Oppressed Human Variety*
(1928; translated by John Lauritsen)

*Kurt Hiller [1885–1972] was a well-known German writer who often
opined in support of socialism and gay rights. This speech, given at the
Second International Congress for Sexual Reform in Copenhagen, had to
be read by Magnus Hirschfeld, as Hiller could not afford to travel to the
event. Hiller defends homosexuality against claims of perversion that had
been recently made by Henri Barbusse and other members of the French
Communist Party.*

HONORABLE PRESIDENT, distinguished members of the Congress!

I thank you for giving me the opportunity to express my
thoughts to you—indirectly; I should have presented them myself
in your midst, had my economic situation not prevented me from
making the trip to Copenhagen.

I wish to use the international forum you have set up to cry
out to the world: From time immemorial there has existed among
all peoples an unusual, but otherwise perfectly worthy, harmless,
guiltless variety of human being, and this variety—as if we were
still living in the darkest Middle Ages—is senselessly and horribly
persecuted by many peoples, following the lead of their legislators,

governments, and courts. Let the intellectual world, the researchers and policy makers of all nations, stand up against this barbarism and demand in the name of humanity: Halt!

The variety of which I speak is that minority of human beings whose love impulses are directed, not towards a member of the other, but rather towards a member of their own sex; these are the so-called homosexuals, Urnings, or inverts. They are outlawed, it is said, because their feelings and acts are "contrary to nature." However, their feelings and acts are rooted in their constitution, components of their character, something dictated to them by their nature. And since the history of all primitive and all civilized peoples demonstrates that such a minority has existed in all ages, then this fact means that we are obligated to recognize this nature as being indeed perfectly natural—shocking perhaps, but nothing that deserves either to be denied or defamed. A phenomenon of nature, that is incomprehensible or discomfiting to the majority, does not cease on that account to be a phenomenon of nature.

Same-sex love is not a mockery of nature, but rather nature at play; and anyone who maintains the contrary—that love, as everyone knows, is intended to serve the propagation of the species, that homosexual or heterosexual potency is squandered on goals other than procreation—fails to consider the superabundance with which Nature in all her largesse wastes semen, millions and billions of times over. As Nietzsche expressed it in *Daybreak*, "Procreation is a frequently occurring accidental result of *one* way of satisfying the sexual drive—it is neither its goal nor its necessary consequence." The theory which would make procreation the "goal" of sexuality is exposed as hasty, simplistic and false by the phenomenon of same-sex love alone. Nature's laws, unlike the laws formulated by the human mind, cannot be violated. The assertion that a specific phenomenon of nature could somehow be "contrary to nature" amounts to pure absurdity. Nevertheless, this absurd claim has persisted for many centuries in literature and in legislation, and even quite celebrated sex educators have come out with this nonsense. Just recently, an internationally renowned spokesman of the European left, Henri Barbusse, exhibited his knowledge and brain power most unfavorably when he answered, in response to a circular enquiry on homosexuality (in the Paris magazine, *Les Marges*, of 15 March 1926): "I believe that this diversion of a natural instinct is, like many other perversions, a sign of the profound social and moral decadence of a certain sector of present-day society. In all eras, decadence has manifested itself in over-refinements and anomalies of the senses, feelings, and emotions."

One must reply to Monsieur Barbusse that this alleged "over-refinement" of which he speaks, uncritically parroting a popular misconception, has always manifested itself just as much at times when a race was on the ascent as when it was in decline; that for example, love between man and youth was no more excluded from the heroic and golden ages of Ancient Greece, than it was from the most illustrious period of Islamic culture, or from the age of Michelangelo; and that a Marxist is making a fool of himself when he tries to connect the homosexuality of the present with the class struggle, by pointing to it as a symptom of the "moral decadence" of "a certain sector" of society, namely the bourgeois sector: as though same-sex love did not occur among proletarians of all kinds—among workers, peasants, employees, little people in all occupations—just as much as among the possessing classes.

The experience of sexologists and psychotherapists proves the contrary. Nature does not stop at any social class when creating her marvelous varieties of human beings. It is true that the proletariat as a rule has less time and means than the propertied class to devote to the pursuit of sexual pleasure, even to the sublime forms of sublimated eroticism; and this is one reason which, among many others, leads—or ought to lead—the fighter for human happiness towards socialism. But this is just as true for the broad mass of proletarians considered heterosexual as for the minority considered homosexual.

The public hears much less about the homosexuality of the modest little people than it does about that of the luxury circles of the big bourgeoisie, but it would be extremely superficial to infer on this basis that homosexuality is some kind of monopoly of the bourgeoisie. One must realize, rather, that the outlawing of same-sex Eros strikes the homosexual proletarian even harder than the homosexual capitalist, because the capitalist has the resources at his disposal to evade it more easily.

At any rate, the homosexually inclined worker owes little gratitude to Monsieur Barbusse when he attacks the alleged "complacency" with which some authors place their "delicate talents" at the service of the homosexual question, "while our old world convulses in terrible economic and social crises," venomously asserting that their doing so "does no honor to this decadent intellectual phalanx" and that it "can only reinforce the contempt which the young and healthy popular force feels for the advocates of this unhealthy and artificial doctrine."

The "terrible economic and social crises" in which the world is "convulsing" apparently prevent Monsieur Barbusse from relinquishing a prejudice he shares with the most backward people of all nations. The Emperor Napoleon and his Chancellor Cambacères were more revolutionary four generations ago, when they freed homosexual acts from the penal code, than this revolutionary of today. Barbusse sings the same moralizing tune on this matter, of which he understands nothing, as the most reactionary ministers in the German government when their "theme" is to draft bills on matters of which they likewise understand nothing. "Contempt," "healthy popular force," "unhealthy doctrine"—we have long heard phrases like these from the conservative and clerical jurists of the Wilhelminian era.

At this moment, when Soviet Russia has abolished the penalties on homosexual acts (per se); when fascism is on the rise, appearing in Italy for the first time in generations; when reaction and progress are locked in furious combat over the homosexual question in Germany and several other countries; along comes Comrade Barbusse, member of the Third International. Unburdened by any relevant knowledge, he delivers a bigoted, agitational tirade against a species of human being that is already sufficiently agitated against, and he unscrupulously stabs in the back those who are waging a good fight on behalf of freedom, even if by its nature the cause is unpopular. I regret that I find it necessary to speak the truth so bluntly to a master those poetry and political-philosophy I once admired; but the higher someone stands, who disseminates false and reactionary theories, the more sharply he must be rebutted, for his theories are all the more dangerous.

It is not true that homosexuality is a sign of "decadence" or something pathological. Men of glowing physical health, of undeniable mental soundness, and of great intellectual powers have been bearers of this inclination—just as often as have been the weak, the unstable, and the inferior. There are inferior, average and superior homosexuals—exactly as there are inferior, average and superior heterosexuals. To belong, not to the rule, not to the "norm," but rather to the exception, to the minority, to the variety, is neither a symptom of degeneration nor of pathology. Likewise, having red hair is neither decadent nor sick. If it is true that there are higher percentages of the mentally weak, the eccentric, the unbalanced, the hypersensitive and the hypertense among homosexuals than among those oriented in the usual way, the blame should not be placed on the predisposition, but rather upon the circumstances in which these people find themselves: one who lives constantly under the onus of attitudes and laws that stamp his inclination as inferior, must be of an unusually robust nature to retain his full worth in every respect. If the terrible weight of contempt and persecution that bears down on homosexuals were to be lifted from them, the neurotic traits within would to the same degree vanish, and then the intrinsic creative worth of their nature, especially the pedagogical ability of which Plato wrote, would come into play.

It is necessary to incorporate homosexuals in the general culture of society, to assign homosexuality a place in society where it can act productively, for it has its own fertility. Hellas, and above all Sparta, understood this and knew how to draw the practical conclusions from this knowledge. But before homosexuality can be assigned this positive and even sublime role in the state, which corresponds to its particular character and at the same time is of service to the state, we must first carry out a negative, liberating and humanitarian action directed against the worst injustice: that the public outlawry, under which this variety suffers, must be abolished in all countries. To be sure, it is not just the penal code that is involved, but it is the penal code that must be dealt with first. Homosexual acts committed by fully competent and mutually consenting adults are still punished in England (one may recall the tragedy of Oscar Wilde); and in the United States, along with Argentina and Chile; in Germany and Austria; in several Scandinavian, East-European and Balkan countries; and also in the German Canton of Switzerland—only homosexual women are for the most part privileged. In these countries, the threat of a long prison sentence is real. The German draft penal code of 1925 provides for a maximum of ten years in the penitentiary!

It is not society in these countries which profits thereby, but rather the tribe of blackmailers and thousands of socially valuable lives are ruined. Despite Monsieur Barbusse, France, and along with France the great majority of Latin countries, no longer have the penalty; likewise the Islamic countries, China and Japan do not have it; and the Soviet Union, as I have already mentioned, has abolished it.

It is clear that socially harmful conduct in the sphere of same-sex love should remain punishable to the same degree as socially harmful conduct in the sphere of opposite-sex love; that therefore the free sexual self-determination of adults and the inexperience of sexually immature youth should be protected by law, and that the misuse of economic or official dependence for lascivious purposes should be forbidden, as well as indecent behavior in public places—with complete parity between heterosexual and homosexual acts. If anyone claims that the homosexual liberation movement would like to see *Carte Blanche* given to unrestrained and anti-social debauchery, or that such liberation would place the interests of the abnormal above the interests of society—then he is lying. The interests of society come first; but I question whether the interests of society demand that human beings be thrown in prison, disgraced and ruined socially, for acts that harm no one, merely because their erotic taste differs from that of the majority. I question whether the interest of society is served when a minority of its members are forced through severe penalties into lifelong sexual abstinence or chronic self-gratification (the situation imposed upon convicts serving life sentences)—a minority which, we know, causes not the slightest harm by following its own nature.

That child molesters or homosexual lust-murderers should be protected is not the thrust of my argument. Prudishness, along with false and monstrous notions about the forms that same-sex love-making takes, prevents a general public discussion of the problem—especially in countries where it is most needed. And even more than prudishness: the apathy of those not personally involved, both in the masses and among the intelligentsia. One must have a great sense of justice and noblesse to take on the cause of a persecuted minority to which one does not personally belong. But fortunately there are still a certain number of people distinguished by such fairness. These people comprehend that an age in which concern for national minorities is so extraordinarily keen and active must find the courage to protect a minority which, to be sure is not an ethnic one, but which can be found in all states, and is especially deserving of protection, since there is no state in the world where they are the majority and with which they, like the national minorities, could identify. International minority rights, which are slowly taking shape, should defend not only the national, the racial and the religious minorities, but also the psycho-biological, the sexual minorities, so long as they are harmless; and if the Second International Congress for Sexual Reform chooses to speak out in favor of these ideas, it would be a courageous act of ethical rationality.

Franklin Kameny

Civil Liberties: A Progress Report
(New York City, 1964)

Dr. Franklin Kameny [born 1925] is an American gay rights activist best known for his successful eighteen-year struggle to overturn the U.S. Civil Service Commission's ban on employing homosexuals. Additionally, Kameny has been an integral part of the gay rights movement in almost all of its efforts throughout the second half of the twentieth century. In this speech, which Kameny gave at a Mattachine Society gathering at Freedom House in New York City, he explains why the gay rights movement is such an important piece of the civil rights movement as a whole.

GOOD EVENING, ladies and gentlemen. It is a pleasure and a privilege to appear before you this evening, as your 100th monthly speaker.

My talk tonight will fall into two major parts. Because I have done and am doing my best to lead my organization—the Mattachine Society of Washington—in directions somewhat different from those traditional to homophile organizations in this country, the first part of my talk will be a presentation of the homophile movement as a civil liberties and social rights action movement, and of the philosophy and rationale behind what I have been trying to do.

I usually try to tailor my talks to my audience and so my talk this evening is directed to some extent to an audience which as I believe you are, is a mixture of both "in-group" and "out-group." And part of it will be directed to those active in the homophile movement.

My approach is one of strong and definite positions, unequivocally held—I feel that the nurture and presentation of controversy are not as virtuous as many in the movement would have them be, nor is the cultivation of an outward neutrality on questions upon which we should be taking a firm, clear, no-nonsense stand.

Let me make it clear at the outset that, like any organization based upon strongly-held beliefs, and composed in its active part of people of strong personality, there exists a considerable range of viewpoint within the Mattachine Society of Washington on many matters directly relevant to the homophile movement. For this reason, the views I express this evening are my own, and are not necessarily those held in any formal sense by the Mattachine Society of Washington.

It seems to me that there are three primary directions in which a homophile organization can go—social service, information and education, and civil liberties—social action. These are complementary, of course, neither mutually exclusive nor competitive, and usually become matters of a difference of emphasis from one organization to another—the placing of the emphasis resulting from a mixture of the setting in which the organization finds itself and the interests and personalities of those leading the particular group.

As I understand it, the Daughters of Bilitis, for example, devotes itself primarily to social service; the Mattachine Society of New York, in the well-established Mattachine tradition, emphasizes the information and education role. The Mattachine Society of Washington, from the outset (because of my own interests, and because in Washington, it seems the clear and obvious direction to take) has placed its emphasis in the area of civil liberties and social action. It is as an exponent of that emphasis that I speak this evening.

My reasons for placing emphasis where I do are the following.

In regard to social services: No *lasting* good can be accomplished by administration of social service *alone*. Let me give an example by analogy. One can supply virtually unlimited amounts of money, food, clothing, and shelter to the poor, but unless one gets to the roots of poverty—the economic system which produces unemployment, the social system which produces lack of education, and the one which over-produces people, etc.—one will accomplish little of lasting value. Similarly, we can refer homosexuals to lawyers, we can find jobs for those who have lost jobs, or have been denied them because of homosexuality, and we can assist them in other ways, but unless and until we get at and eliminate the discrimination and prejudice which underlie—and, in fact, which *are*—the homosexuals' problems, we will accomplish nothing of lasting value, either, and our job will go on literally without end.

Obviously we cannot easily turn away people now in need with the argument that we are working in order that those in the future will not need; so there is clearly a place in the homophile movement for the social services—and the Mattachine Society of Washington does its share—but only, I feel, to supplement work of a more fundamental nature, dealing with changes of attitude, prejudice and policy.

We come next to the area of information and education. While this is important, I feel that any movement which relies solely upon an intellectually-directed program of information and education, no matter how extensive, to change well-entrenched, emotionally-based attitudes, is doomed to disappointment. The Negro tried for 90 years to achieve his purposes by a program of information and education. His achievements in those 90 years, while by no means nil, were nothing compared to those of the past 10 years, when he tried a vigorous civil liberties, social action approach and gained his goals thereby.

The prejudiced mind, and that is what we are fighting, is not penetrated by information and is not educable. This has been shown in a number of studies of the mental processes associated with prejudice, and has been confirmed by a recent study which showed that tolerance is only slightly promoted by more information: that communication of facts is generally ineffectual against predispositions: that prejudiced opinions, attitudes, and beliefs, usually change only when people are forced to change.

The prejudice against homosexuality is primarily one of an emotional commitment, not an intellectual one; and appeals based upon fact and reason will, for the most part, not be effective.

Where a program of information and education *will* be useful and very important is in presenting our position to that minority of the majority who are potentially our allies anyway, but who have not thought about the matter before—such as the clergy, as just one of a number of examples—who are looked to as leaders by the masses of people.

Even there, however, a vigorous and outgoing program is necessary. Let me illustrate this point with an anecdote. Late in 1962, when the Mattachine Society of Washington was about a year old and had begun to establish itself in the homophile movement by more than its mere existence, I wrote letters to all of the other homophile organizations in the country introducing our group and describing some of the endeavors in which we were then engaged. I mentioned our dealings with the Washington chapter of the ACLU. One of the organizations wrote back, saying that they too had contacted their local ACLU affiliate, and that ACLU representatives had spoken to their membership on several occasions. I replied by saying that representatives of the ACLU had never addressed our membership, but representatives of the Mattachine Society of Washington had addressed the ACLU's membership. I think the difference is illustrative of my point and is important. It has served us exceedingly well.

Information and education, yes—but *not* to inform and educate us. The homophile movement does not, I feel, exist in any major degree for the edification of its own members. In its information and education role, it exists primarily to inform and to educate the public. We should appear before the public in the role of authorities on questions of homosexuality—as indeed we are. I am truly pleased to see growing, particularly on the East Coast, a strong trend toward the bringing of the talks, the lectures, the discussions, outside our own group, and before other groups—before the heterosexual public.

This brings us to the area of civil liberties and social action. Here, we get into an area in which we are engaging in what is fundamentally down-to-earth, grass-roots, occasionally tooth-and-nail politics. We are dealing with emotions of people, and the policies of officialdom, and our methods must be in accord with this.

Let me digress briefly. Official policies—laws, regulations, etc., on the one hand and popular opinion and prejudice on the other hand, interact strongly and circularly. This is obvious. It is therefore obvious, too, that if we work almost infinitely long to change public attitudes and are successful in doing so, or wait for them to evolve, then after another long wait, we might see laws and official policies change. The reverse process is much faster, and much more efficient and is especially suited to a group located, as mine is, in Washington.

The current issue of *Scientific American* magazine has an article which bears directly upon this matter. In a study of changes of attitudes on integration in various parts of the country it is pointed out "that official action has *preceded* public sentiment, and public sentiment has then attempted to accommodate itself to the new situation." This lesson should not be lost upon us.

Prejudiced official attitudes and policies reinforce private discrimination. The private employer, for example, may or may not hire homosexuals, if the government *does* hire them; he will *not* hire them if the government does *not*. That is over-simplified, of course, but in terms of large-scale policies and practices, it is true.

For these reasons, lightly touched upon here, I feel that the primary direction of endeavor and the one likely to be most fruitful should be the changing of the attitudes and policies of those who are, or to whom the community looks, as constituted authority. Wherever discrimination is officially sponsored, it is amenable to attack within the framework of administrative and judicial procedure. This has been the backbone (but let it be emphasized, not the totality) of our approach in Washington; and I would very much like to see such an approach extended elsewhere, including New York.

I would suggest that here in New York you have at least one beautiful example of the kind of situation which needs this sort of approach, and which is much more fundamental than would appear upon first thought. I refer to the continued closing of gay bars. This seems to me to be an obvious infringement upon the right of the homosexual citizen to freely associate, to assemble, and to make use of public accommodations of his own choice on a basis of equality with other citizens. I have suggested that (strategy, tactics, and timing permitting) this is a matter which a group such as Mattachine Society of New York might well take up. I am told that it is difficult to get a bar owner who will cooperate. *This is not a matter for the bar owners. This is a matter for homosexuals.* The lawsuits which brought an end to school segregation were not initiated by schools which wished to integrate; they were brought by Negro school children who wished to attend. The parallel is valid.

One homosexual or several homosexuals in a group, *as homosexuals,* and as potential or actual patrons of otherwise legal establishments which, by stated public policy, they may not patronize, should bring the necessary suit against the proper officials. I feel that it is very much the role of the homophile organizations to encourage, to support, and to create such test cases.

I will extract an item from the second part of my talk to illustrate our position in Washington. We have an all-night restaurant, patronized by numbers of homosexuals. One night the police came in and requested a show of identification of all those who they thought were homosexuals. One of our members, well-coached in his rights, refused to show identification (citizens do not have to do so). He was arrested and I had to bail him out in the wee hours of one Sunday morning. Not only did the case go to court, with the support, elicited by us, of the ACLU, but more important, a formal complaint was made to the Police Department by the ACLU about certain aspects of the case. The Mattachine Society of Washington, on its own, also made a complaint—not only to the Police Department, but to the President of the Board of Commissioners, our closest equivalent to a mayor. In our complaint we pointed out that homosexuals, whether singly or in groups, are entitled to the same use of public accommodations of their choice as are all other citizens, and that the Mattachine Society of Washington was prepared to take all measures legally within its power to ensure that those rights were not infringed upon. A similar letter was sent to Senator Morse, who takes an interest in police practices in the District of Columbia. We have received replies indicating that the matter is being pursued. We intend to follow it up.

It is in matters of this sort that a civil rights philosophy is, I think, effective.

Returning, however, to matters of rationale of approach—I feel that in going before the public, it is absolutely necessary to be prepared to take definite, unequivocal positions upon supposedly controversial matters. We should have a clear, explicit, consistent viewpoint and we should not be timid in presenting it.

In presenting our view to a generally prejudiced public, we are not presenting data to a scientific body. If one presents to a scientific audience nine points in favor of a particular viewpoint, and a tenth point which is doubtful, the scientific audience will grant that the viewpoint has a 90% chance of being correct. Present the same nine points to a person of prejudiced mind, and the first nine points will slide off, as water off a duck's back, and in seeking to retain his prejudices he will seize upon the uncertainty in the tenth, and will say "See, even they agree with me, so I must be right." And become more confirmed in his beliefs than before. Thus it behooves us to take and to present clear, explicit, firm positions.

There are those in the movement who seem to feel that whenever controversy exists, we should be impelled to impartially present both or all sides of the question. I disagree. Having examined the issue, and decided which side is, in our view, correct and consistent with the aims of the homophile movement, we should then present that side alone, presenting the other only to refute it, and as not having equal merit with the view we espouse. We should certainly not sponsor the presentation of opposing views. The

Democrats don't present the views of the Republicans as having equal merit with theirs. Our opponents will do a fully adequate job of presenting their views, and will not return us the favor of presenting ours; we gain nothing in virtue by presenting theirs, and only provide the enemy—and let us not think of them as less than an enemy—with ammunition to be used against us.

We are not dealing with scientists; let us not employ the scientific method where it is not applicable. To do so is naïve and unrealistic to an almost suicidal degree.

As our dealings with some of the government officials in Washington have indicated, we are dealing with an opposition which manifests itself—not always, but not infrequently—as a ruthless, unscrupulous foe who will give no quarter and to whom any standards of fair play are meaningless. Let us respond realistically. We are not playing a gentlemanly game of tiddly-winks or croquet or chess. An impractical, theoretical intellectualism is utterly unrealistic and can be completely self-destructive in this context.

Now, a few particular points. My starting point is one now well accepted among the homophile organizations, although still novel elsewhere—that the homosexuals make up a minority group comparable to other, what might be called sociological minorities, such as the Negroes, the Jews, etc. I think that this should be explicitly justified, however, since direct challenges to the concept are frequently posed.

I feel that a little consideration will show that aside from the obvious statistical basis, a minority group in the sense in which we speak, must possess four characteristics.

First, the members must possess, in common, some single characteristic or closely related group of characteristics, but otherwise be heterogenous.

Second, on account of this characteristic, but *not* in reasonable, rational or logical consequence of it, the majority about them must look down upon the members of the group, and must discriminate adversely against them.

There is a third facet of minority-majority group relations which is a little more subtle, but which I think is always present in regard to a group which is a sociological minority. The consequences of the faults and the sins of the individual members of the minority are visited upon all members of the minority. Let a white, heterosexual, Anglo-Saxon Protestant commit a crime, and he alone is blamed. Let a Jew, a Negro, or a homosexual commit a crime, and epithets and blame are depicted against all members of his minority. Let a few members of the majority be personally objectionable or ridiculous to large numbers of people, and the reactions to their offensiveness will be directed against them individually. Let a few members of a minority group be offensive or ridiculous to large numbers of people, and a stereotype will be created which will be applied indiscriminately to all those known to be members of the minority group. This is true of the Negro and Jewish minorities; I hardly need to point out that it is also true of the homosexual minority.

A fourth criterion for the establishment of a sociological minority group is a feeling on the part of members of the minority of cohesiveness, of belonging, and of identity among themselves. This does not have to imply a feeling of belonging to an organization or movement—much as the members of the homophile movement might like all homosexuals to feel—but a feeling of kinship to others whom they know to be members of this minority group. This feeling is clearly present among homosexuals, and strongly so.

With this as a starting point, I look upon the homophile organizations as playing for the homosexual minority the same role as is played by the NAACP or CORE [Congress of Racial Equality] for the Negro minority.

We cannot ask for our rights as a minority group, and I will elaborate briefly upon just what it is we are asking for; we cannot ask for our rights from a position of inferiority or from a position, shall I say, as less than whole human beings. I feel that the entire homophile movement, in terms of any accomplishments beyond merely ministering to the needy, is going to stand or fall upon the question of whether or not homosexuality is a sickness, and upon our taking a firm stand on it. I feel that *The New York Times* article of last December 17, and the recent *New York Academy of Medicine Report* have made this abundantly clear. The Question arises every time there is serious discussion of homosexuality, and I feel that an unequivocal position must be taken.

I do not intend this evening to go into a lengthy or detailed discussion of this question. Suffice it to say for the moment that a reading of the so-called authorities on this matter shows an appalling incidence of loose reasoning, of poor research, of supposedly generally applicable conclusions being derived from an examination of non-representative samplings, of conclusions being incorporated into initial assumptions, and vice versa, with the consequent circular reasoning. A case in point is the recent, much relied upon study by Bieber. Not only were the homosexuals in his study all patients of his, and therefore, *a priori,* disturbed, but he makes the statement: "All psychoanalytic theories assume that adult homosexuality is pathological." Obviously if one assumes that homosexuality is pathological, then one will discover that homosexuality is a sickness, and that homosexuals are disturbed, just as, if one assumes that two plus two equal five, one is likely to discover that three plus one are equal to five. In both instances, the assumption requires proof before it can be seriously entertained.

There seems to be no valid evidence to show that homosexuality, *per se,* is a sickness. In view of the absence of such valid evidence, the simple fact that the suggestion of sickness has been made is no reason for entertaining it seriously, or for abandoning the view that homosexuality is not a sickness, but merely a liking or preference similar to and fully on a par with heterosexuality. Accordingly, I take the position unequivocally that, until and unless valid, positive evidence shows otherwise, homosexuality, *per se,* is neither a sickness, a defect, a disturbance, a neurosis, a psychosis, nor a malfunction of any sort.

I will go further, and say that I feel so strongly that the rationale for the homophile movement rests, and rests heavily upon this position, that should evidence arise to show conclusively that this position is in error, I shall give serious thought to leaving the movement. I do not anticipate that I shall ever need to do so.

Another question which has a way of intruding itself upon any general discussion of homosexuality—much less so, of late, than it formerly did, although it still is the basis for the Federal Government's approach to the question—is that of morality and immorality. It is a point upon which I have rarely heard a straight, direct statement of position from persons in the homophile movement—even when expressing publicly their own views.

Matters of morality, of course, are ones clearly of personal opinion and individual religious belief so that, except for an affirmation of the right of all individuals to adopt their own viewpoints upon those matters, without penalty therefore, and without the official imposition of orthodox views, the homophile movement would be in error in proscribing a position.

However for myself, I take the stand that not only is homosexuality, whether by mere inclination or by overt act, not immoral, but that homosexual acts engaged in by consenting adults are moral, in a positive and real sense, and are right, good and desirable, both for the individual participants and for the society in which they live.

There is another point which comes up frequently in discussions of homosexuality: the matter of the origins of homosexuality and the possibility of re-orientation to heterosexuality. While, as a person dealing in all aspects of homosexuality, I find that these questions are ones of some passing interest; from the viewpoint of civil liberties and social rights, these questions interest me *not at all*.

I do not see the NAACP and CORE worrying about which chromosome and gene produces a black skin or about the possibility of bleaching the Negro. I do not see any great interest on the part of the B'nai B'rith Anti-Defamation League in the possibility of solving problems of anti-semitism by converting Jews to Christianity.

In all of these minority groups, we are interested in obtaining rights for our respective minorities, *as* Negroes, *as* Jews, and *as* homosexuals. Why we are Negroes, Jews or homosexuals, is totally irrelevant, and whether we can be changed to whites, Christians, or heterosexuals is equally irrelevant.

Further, as implied a moment ago, I look upon the assumption that it is somehow desirable that we be converted to heterosexuality (with the implied assumption that homosexuality is an inferior status) as being presumptuously arrogant and an assault upon our right to be ourselves on a par with those around us, as would be similar attempts for example, to convert Jews to Christianity—something which, for just that reason, has become unfashionable in this country.

There is one final point of basic approach, before I become somewhat more specific—and this is a somewhat subtle one, one which is difficult to express clearly. In reading through many statements put out by the homophile movement, there is easily perceptible a defensive tone—a lightly-veiled feeling that homosexuality really is inferior to heterosexuality but that, since we have to live with it, it must be made the best of. While I do not, of course, take the ridiculous viewpoint discussed in the recent *New York Academy of Medicine Report* that homosexuality and homosexuals are superior to heterosexuality and heterosexuals, I am unwilling to grant even the slightest degree of inferiority: I look upon homosexuality as something in no way shameful or intrinsically undesirable.

Now, from the civil liberties and social rights viewpoint, just what do we want? I feel that we want, basically, what all other minority groups want and what every American citizen has the right to request and to expect—in fact, to demand: To be judged and to be treated, each upon his own merits as an individual and only on those criteria truly relevant to a particular situation, not upon irrelevant criteria, as homosexuality always is, having to do only with the harmless conduct of our private lives. We wish, AS HOMOSEXUALS, to be rid of the contempt directed against us by our fellow citizens—contempt which exists without reason, which serves only to render contemptible those manifesting it, and which is reinforced and perpetuated by present official attitude and policy—and it is the latter which, in great measure, is the target of a civil rights endeavor.

In short, as homosexuals we want (to quote from a portion of the statement of purpose of the Mattachine Society of Washington) "the right, as human beings, to develop our full potential and dignity, and the right, as citizens, to be allowed to make our maximum contribution to the society in which we live." These rights are ours in fact, though we are currently denied them in practice.

I feel that with due regard for strategy and tactics, we must take a bold, strong, uncompromising initiative in working for these rights; that the established framework of authority, constituted and otherwise, must be challenged directly by every lawful means at hand.

There will, of course, be reactions to any such attempts—both *The New York Times* article and the *New York Academy of Medicine Report,* to mention but two of several possibilities, are examples of the heterosexual backlash which is a parallel to the white backlash in the Negro rights movement—and we can expect them with somewhat increasing intensity. Such backlash, too, must be faced squarely and responded to fully. Most important, that such backlash may occur must not be allowed to act as a deterrent to further action.

It would be possible to discourse on these matters at greater length, but time is getting on, and my topic of major concern is the Washington homophile scene, so I'll proceed to the second part of my talk.

The Mattachine Society of Washington has a short history; the organization was founded only two and a half years ago—so it is reasonable to first review all of the organization's significant activities to date, and then proceed to proposed projects and those already underway.

Our first major project (in August two years ago) was the sending of a letter to every member of Congress, to the President and his Cabinet, to other members of the Executive Branch, and to members of the Judicial Branch of the Federal Government, as well as to officials of the Government of the District of Columbia. This letter informed the recipients of our existence and goals. It was accompanied by a copy of our statement of purpose and by a

news release asking for changes in Federal policy toward homosexuals, in the areas of Federal Civil Service employment, the issu-
ance of security clearances, and policies of the Armed Forces.

As might be expected, the results were few but not nil. We
received favorable replies from Congressman Ryan of the 20th
District of Manhattan's West Side, and Congressman Nix of the
4th District in Central Philadelphia. We visited the offices and
spoke to Nix in person.

We also received from Mr. John W. Macy, Jr., the Chairman of
the U.S. Civil Service Commission and a man whom I consider
to be the Federal equivalent, for our minority, of Alabama's Governor Wallace or Mississippi's ex-Governor Barnett, an explicit
statement of policy which has served us well.

This mailing also led to an explanatory conference at the Penta-
gon with the Defense Department's top security officials in regard
to policies on security clearances for homosexuals.

In the following year, we approached the Selective Service officials, which resulted in a conference with General Hershey, head
of the Selective Service, in regard to the question of confidential-
ity of replies to draft questionnaires. The information involved is
not open, under any circumstances, to private citizens but *is* open
to other Federal and state officials. We objected to this.

This project has moved slowly over to the Department of the
Army. The Office of the Secretary of the Army has indicated to us
that they are neither willing to alter their policy, to restrict disclo-
sure of information only to those in the Department of the Army
who require it for administration of the draft regulations, nor are
they willing to engage in discussion of the matter with us.

This being the case, and acting individually and on my own
in my capacity as an independent, private citizen, I wish to state
publicly, that I encourage anyone, homosexual or heterosexual,
who is subject to the draft, and who feels strongly about the con-
fidentiality of the information he supplies, or about the Army's
savage policies toward homosexuals, to refuse, outright and firmly,
on principle, to give any response at all to the question asked at
the physical examination, as to whether or not one has or has had

homosexual tendencies. This refusal should be based upon two grounds:

- That this is information which is of no proper concern to the Government of the United States under any circumstances whatever, and which the Government does not' have the need to know, and;
- That this information is open to improper persons (i.e., the FBI, Civil Service Commission investigators, state officials, etc.).

If anyone wishes to make a test case out of this, I will be pleased to offer every possible assistance. We can make a forum out of the court room and get our grievances on these matters before the public.

Another area of our Society's activity was the celebrated matter of the Congressional Bill HR-5990. In order to raise funds and in compliance with the laws of the District of Columbia, the Mattachine Society of Washington, in 1962, obtained a license under the so-called Charitable Solicitations Act, allowing us to solicit for funds.

This came to the attention of Rep. John Dowdy (Democrat of East Texas) who is one of the banes of the existence of the Government of the District of Columbia. As chairman of a subcommittee of the House of Representatives' Committee on the District of Columbia, he introduced a bill, HR-5990, requiring that every organization registering be found affirmatively to contribute to the health, the welfare, and the morals of the District of Columbia, in the expectation that we could not qualify. The second portion of the bill, later deleted, explicitly revoked' the certificate of registration held by the Mattachine Society of Washington.

We alerted the District of Columbia government and the local ACLU and requested hearings on the bill. The hearings were held. The District of Columbia government testified for three-quarters of an hour against the bill: I testified for four and a half hours; our vice-president testified for one-half hour; and an ACLU representative testified for an hour. The D.C. Republican Committee sent in a letter opposing the bill, as did others, and an editorial opposing the bill appeared in *The Washington Post*.

Rep. Dowdy expected to make something of a circus of the hearings at our expense. Instead, we received much favorable publicity, became well-established in the eyes of the Government of the District of Columbia as a reputable group, and, in general, reaped such a favorable harvest from the hearings that we seriously considered citing Dowdy as the Federal official who did the most in 1963 for the homophile movement.

In the autumn of last year under pressure from Dowdy, the Government of the District of Columbia called a hearing to revoke our license. At my suggestion, our attorney pointed out to the District of Columbia's attorney that this hearing was not going to be a bed of roses for the District, because we intended to ask each member of the hearing board whether he was sufficiently unprejudiced against homosexuals to render an unbiased decision. If he were not, then the hearing, and any revocation stemming from it, would be invalid. If he were, he could count on pressure from the Dowdys to deprive him of his job.

At the District Government's request, a conference was held a few days later among the lawyers, in order to find a way out of the situation without a hearing. It was found that, according to one provision of the Charitable Solicitation Act, we didn't need a license anyway, so we turned it in with the clear proviso, stated in a letter, that our fund-raising activities would continue without restriction.

The newspapers picked up the story in somewhat distorted form. We wrote a letter which was printed, again stating that our fund-raising activities were not restricted in any way and closing with the sentence: "Solicitations for funds continue actively."

Further Congressional hearings were held in January, then in March in a report which very nicely quoted some of our purposes, the House District of Columbia Committee favorably reported the bill out to the floor. We immediately alerted the ACLU who sent telegrams to 40 congressmen; we also sent telegrams. Two weeks later a minority report opposing the bill was issued by 9 of the 24 committee members, including Rep. Multer of Brooklyn.

The minority report started out by saying: "In our judgment, HR-5990 is an ill-considered, unnecessary, unwise, and unconstitutional measure. It is a danger to the people of the District of Columbia and should be rejected."

The publication of this report was a necessary pre-requisite under House procedures for full-scale debate of the bill on the House floor. At that time, an editorial appeared in *The Washington Post* titled "Piety By Fiat" and referred to an "oddly inept little bill by that Master of Morality, Rep. Dowdy." It closed by suggesting that Rep. Dowdy's bill be consigned to oblivion.

District of Columbia bills can come up on so-called District Mondays (the 2nd and 4th Mondays of each month). I have called the Capitol each Monday: the bill has not come up. The Chairman of the local ACLU has stated publicly that he considers it dead.

In March of 1963, we presented to the U.S. Civil Rights Commission a 9-page statement entitled "Discrimination Against the Employment of Homosexuals" and we testified at hearings held at that time by the Commission.

At our instigation, the Washington ACLU's Committee on Discrimination has devoted a considerable portion of its time to the problems of homosexuals. Most recently, the Washington ACLU has adopted, as an item of its policy, a statement strongly opposing the U.S. Civil Service Commission's policies against the employment of homosexuals.

We have done our best to encourage the bringing of court test cases against the Government in the areas mentioned before: U.S. civil service employment, security clearances, and military discharges, in an effort to bring about changes in Federal policies on these matters. If anyone here this evening has a potential case against the Federal Government in those areas, I would be most interested in hearing about it and I encourage its being brought to court. We have several cases now in progress.

In May of 1963, for the first time within the memory of anyone, a gay bar in Washington was raided. I spent much of the
month of June last year collecting affidavits from those arrested. A
formal complaint was filed by the Mattachine Society of Washington against the Police Department. A conference was held involving high police officials and Mattachine Society of Washington
officials. As a consequence, I don't think that any more gay bars
in Washington will be raided.

In December of last year, within a very short time, two cases
of attempted blackmail were brought to our attention. We took
both cases to the head of the so-called Morals Division of the
Metropolitan Police Department. They were handled tactfully and
with a minimum of embarrassment. One of the cases resulted in a
mid-afternoon arrest of the blackmailer in a downtown restaurant
complete with all the trappings of a TV melodrama, including
marked money, envelopes filled with newspaper clippings instead
of bills, pre-arranged signals to the police and so forth. The blackmailer is now in prison.

Following these cases *The Washington Post* printed a letter from
our Society commending, on behalf of the Washington homosexual community, the head of the Morals Division and his chief
subordinate for their handling of these cases. I am quite sure that
they never expected a commendation from that source.

In other areas of activity, we have, as has the Mattachine Society
of New York, set up a professional referral service—doctors, lawyers, psychiatrists, clergymen—for homosexuals in need.

At our initiative, a series of conferences on venereal disease has
been held with District Public Health Service officials. Our VD
pamphlet, printed by the District of Columbia, is soon to come
out. A major portion of the work in distributing it will be the
responsibility of the Mattachine Society of Washington. A TV
broadcast on the subject is planned soon with Mattachine Society
of Washington participation.

Mattachine Society of Washington representatives have appeared
on two hour-long radio programs in Washington, one in Philadelphia, and a two-hour TV broadcast in Chicago.

That, in hasty summary, brings up-to-date the accounting of the Society's past activities. We have a number of projects under way and some which have been proposed.

We are considering approaching all of the various District of Columbia licensing boards to inquire about their policies in the licensing for various occupations and professions of persons known to be homosexual. We are also considering approaching the bar and medical associations in the same fashion.

In a similar vein, we are considering approaching the local universities to inquire as to their policies toward homosexual students and staff—I might point out, by way of digression, that in this country an individual known to be a homosexual would find it more difficult to get an education, at any level, in the schools of his choice (or, in fact, in any school at all)—than would a Negro in the South or a Native in the Union of South Africa.

Our approach to the problem of employment of homosexuals who have lost jobs on account of homosexuality is somewhat different from that taken by the Mattachine Society of New York. You have here, in a certain sense, placed yourself—non-remuneratively, of course—in the employment agency business. We choose not to do so. Therefore we are about to send a letter to every employment agency in the greater Washington area, pointing out to them that a problem exists, that there are competent people looking for work, that they—the agencies—have their fingers on the employers in a fashion and to an extent to which we never could have, and asking for their cooperation—with no remuneration to come to us, of course—in finding jobs for these people, if we send them to the agencies. We hope for at least some favorable responses.

In an attempt to broaden the scope of the project, and to tie it in more closely with a civil rights viewpoint, we are also writing similarly to the largest employers in the District of Columbia area, in order to call attention to the existence of the problem.

A proposed project has to do with the publication of two leaflets. One will deal with the rights of and the procedures to be followed by persons arrested. It will stress the point—as true in New York City as in the District of Columbia and as little realized here as there—that persons arrested *do not* have to tell the police where they work or anything else for that matter.

The second leaflet will deal with methods for the handling of Federal investigations and interrogations—FBI, Civil Service, military investigators, etc.—dealing with homosexuality. In view of the obviously harmful effects to the whole country of present Federal policies on homosexuality in their needlessly depriving the nation of the service of competent citizens, it is the patriotic duty of every citizen to do his best in the interests of his country, to resist, to flout, to thwart, to render totally ineffective such investigations and interrogations of homosexuals. Questions on homosexuality, homosexuals, etc., are never the proper concern of the Government and should not be answered. One is never required to answer such questions under any conditions—you don't even have to give FBI investigators and others the time of day—and you shouldn't. The leaflet will advise on these matters.

We have formed a Research Committee now engaged in a number of projects related to the gathering of published information for the Society's own internal use. In addition, it has two major projects just starting and a third proposed. The proposed project comes to us from the local ACLU, and has to do with Federal employees who have been fired. One of the other two projects is a questionnaire to be sent to all the psychiatrists in the area, asking for information on their views on, and approaches to, matters having to do with homosexuals and homosexuality.

The third—and by far the most important of these projects—has to do with blackmail.

One of the most successful brainwashing jobs in human history has been that done by our Federal Government on the American public—including all too many in the homosexual community—in convincing them, to the point that it has become part of American folklore, that (1) all homosexuals are poor security risks because of susceptibility to blackmail; and (2) that exclusion is the only remedy. We don't believe either of these.

We are thus preparing a survey of the homosexual community

on various aspects of the question of blackmail, its prevalence, and the susceptibility of individual homosexuals to it. As far as I know, no one has ever done this before and the homophile organizations obviously can do it better than anyone else. It should provide definite, publishable data to help dispel some of the myths upon which the Government bases some of its policies.

We come now to the last of our current areas of major endeavor, religion. Last December, I gave a talk, followed by discussion, to part of the congregation of Temple Sinai, one of the reformed Jewish congregations in Washington. The talk was well received.

In January, just before one of the radio broadcasts which I mentioned earlier, one of our members telephoned every Unitarian minister in the greater Washington area to tell them of the broadcast; shortly thereafter he sent them a letter, including a copy of Cory's *The Homosexual in America*. This resulted in a sermon by one of the ministers. The sermon was titled "Civil Liberties and the Homosexual" and couldn't have been more satisfactory if I had written it myself. The sermon was followed by two discussion groups—both well attended—at which I was asked to preside.

Subsequently, with the member just mentioned as chairman, I formed a new committee—our Committee on Approaches to the Clergy—which has informally approached perhaps two dozen clergymen of several faiths and denominations, with a considerable and gratifying degree of favorable response. The Committee's bases of approach are two—of equal emphasis. First, we feel that the homosexual finds himself rejected by almost every religious body to the loss and detriment both of the religious bodies and of the homosexuals. We seek to remedy this by working for closer integration of the homosexuals with the religious life of their community.

Second, we wish to enlist the aid of the clergy in our battle for civil rights.

Our committee has drawn up a formal statement of purpose, which, in its present proposed form, pleases me greatly. This very nicely covers all three directions of endeavor discussed above. We plan to send this statement of purpose, our Society's statement of purpose, and a covering letter to the entire clergy of the greater Washington area asking for their assistance and inquiring about their interest in participating in a conference with us.

Most recently, at his initiative, I had lunch with a high official of the Methodists' national headquarters in Washington (we have had very favorable responses from the Methodists). He had just come from a retreat in the San Francisco area, attended by members of the clergy and the homophile movement. He indicated to my pleasure that he felt that we in Washington had done far more in the direction of making contact with the local clergy than had all of the West Coast groups. He was completely with us and wished to assist. He is now rounding up a group of sympathetic ministers of a variety of faiths to meet with us in the very near future. He will try to appear on the program of our forthcoming ECHO conference.

In that connection, I might mention in passing, that the Methodists will have their 5-day national conference in Washington at the same time as the 1964 ECHO conference. Informal plans are now afoot to explore the possibility of some sort of coordination.

I feel that these activities with religious leaders are of the utmost importance because the commitment of most people to their religion and to the leaders thereof is an emotional one. They will follow the lead taken by a minister where they will not follow the intellectual lead set by other leaders and persons in positions of constituted authority. If we can get any substantial portion of the clergy to support us—and a surprising number do—and to support us openly and actively, we can go a very long way, very quickly, toward remedying some of the situations in our regard which are so badly in need of remedy.

That completes a quick accounting of our activities, past, present, and proposed, in all three areas—civil liberties and social rights—information and education—and social service. I hope that the pressures of a somewhat hasty preparation have not made this presentation too unclear, too perfunctory, or too uninteresting.

Jack Nichols

Why I Joined the Movement
(Bucknell University, Pennsylvania, 1967)

Jack Nichols [1938–2005] was an American gay rights activist known as an ardent challenger of the psychiatric theory that homosexuality is a pathological condition, as well as for his role in the founding and development of the Mattachine Societies of Washington, D.C., and Florida.

WHY DID I join the movement to equalize the status of the homosexual? Because I found out that there were rewards. When I stand up in a positive fashion for my own rights I feel self-respect, self-knowledge, and self-confidence. I see that it's helpful when homosexuals stand up for their own rights and take their destiny into their own hands, trying to make a world for themselves that's free of fear, confusion and discrimination.

There is something to be said for casting aside one's fears and confronting the forces of darkness and despair with a healthy vigor. People who work in our movement can't help but benefit from putting their focus on human freedom and dignity.

The effects of discrimination which have reigned over homosexual people are subtly pernicious. In centuries past homosexuals were burned at [the] stake. The dry sticks thrown at their feet were called "faggots." That's [the] origin of that pejorative word.

It may be argued that homosexuals can avoid such pitfalls

without belonging to the Homophile Movement. True. But it is also true that homosexuals must be made of the strongest stuff if they are not to fall prey to insidious confusions that trickle into their minds from an ocean of misunderstandings.

The Homophile Movement to which I belong gives to the homosexual constant awareness of his humanity, of his oneness with the rest of mankind.

It makes him realize that homosexuality should mean no more than left-handedness and that he is a full member of the human race.

These are just a few of the rewards the Homophile Movement grants to those in its ranks. There is also the satisfaction of doing a job never done before. And there is the joy of collaborating with my fellows on projects bringing comfort and hope, aid and solace to millions who have never heard of this movement or who are unable to align themselves although they may hope every day for its success.

Without this movement, what do we find? Look first at the masses of young homosexuals; often bewildered, uninformed, searching for guidance, wondering about their inner feelings, and fighting what Edward Carpenter called "a solitary and really serious inner struggle." A veil of complete silence has been drawn over the subject of homosexuality and this often leads to the most painful misunderstandings.

Look at the agonized face of a parent as he or she learns for the first time the "dreadful" secret of an offspring. Here is an area in which many homosexuals are painfully sensitive. To see the faces of those we love contorted in disbelief, dismay, revulsion, or rejection and anger, is an experience all too common among those who have, in one way or another, revealed life's facts to parents.

The Homophile Movement works toward breaking down not only the prejudices affecting young homosexuals and their parents, but also those which affect homosexuals throughout their lives. When the homosexual community itself stops believing the nonsense that society has been proclaiming, the Movement will have begun to accomplish its goals.

Dr. Wardell B. Pomeroy, co-author of the Kinsey report, states that when homosexuals "are called nuts and neurotics and goofers by therapists, immoral by the clergy, criminals by lawyers and judges, and perverts and child molesters by the public" they need a very "special kind of faith in themselves" and "faith in their fellow man." The Homophile Movement exists to give that faith to its members and to those who share, without being members, its aspirations for a brighter future.

The Homophile Movement has distinct roots in the American dream. It is, in great measure, a social protest movement, but these words alone do not describe it adequately. It is another chapter in the Book of Freedom, asking as it does for the rights of the individual, for the sanctity of privacy in an area—sexual behavior—which is certainly the most personal of concerns.

In a sense, the Homophile Movement is thus protecting not only homosexuals but [also] all people resenting the intrusion of government, employers, and others who pry into their private lives seeking excuses for condemnation and discrimination.

There was a time not long ago when private employers felt free to discriminate against citizens, to hire and fire them on the basis of political beliefs, religion, or race. Today such employers are thought to be misguided, if not immoral, but we live in a nation where an individual's private sexual behavior behind the closed doors of his own home is still considered relevant to employment.

In the Great Society this nation is building, the Homophile Movement is lending new meaning to the primacy of the individual, protesting the ever-watchful eye of Big Brother while it demands freedom of assembly, freedom of the press, and of the right of a person to be the sovereign of his thoughts and feelings.

Homosexuals are mistreated by officialdom not because of what they have done—their actions—but for their inclinations. No policy could be further from the principles on which this country is founded. To dismiss a man, to hound him through the remainder of his life for his thoughts and feelings are the tactics of totalitarianism. A person joining the Homophile Movement is waging war on the growing tendency of officialdom to judge men and women by their private sexual inclinations. This person will help protect fundamental freedoms.

Adlai Stevenson used to say that "the American Revolution is never complete. America is a continuing revolution." The many men and women who annually march in front of Independence Hall on July 4 to remind America of the plight of the homosexual, contribute peacefully and lawfully to the meaning of the Revolution from which American principles developed.

Two heterosexuals stood watching the protest. "It's terrible," said one to the other. His friend turned to him and said, "At last I'm convinced that freedom in this country is meaningful. It makes me realize that America is really going somewhere."

The Homophile Movement belongs to the revolution with which Jefferson allied himself when he swore "eternal hostility against every form of tyranny over the mind of man." There is no tyranny more morbid than that dictating to love and affection and no slave more pitiful than he who succumbs to such dictation.

Sex is a fundamental human need. Those who do not interfere with the rights of others and who pursue this need privately should be protected from interference.

Those people concerned with the meaning of America, longing to build a truly great society, will protest official sexual inspections and official approval of sexual desires and inclinations. They will realize that support of the Homophile Movement is an important way of curbing and stopping such tyranny.

Sally Gearhart

The Lesbian and God-the-Father, or, All the Church Needs
Is a Good Lay ... On Its Side
(Berkeley, California, February 1972)

Sally Miller Gearhart [born 1931] is an American writer, educator, and political activist best known for her lesbian-themed science fiction novels and her dedication to the gay rights movement. In this speech, which she gave at the Pacific School of Religion at Berkeley, Gearhart argues that the church is beyond reform when it comes to homosexuality, and must be either deserted or destroyed.

OF THE host of things I'd like to share with you, a few at least bear mention.

I could speak with you about the twelve specific references to "homosexuality" in the Bible, about the misinterpretations that have been put upon them, about the fact that only one of those references includes any suggestion of female homosexuality.

Or, I might use a feature-article approach on "Lesbians I Have Known In The Church" (and still know). I doubt that many of you would be shocked at personal or experiential estimates of the number of lesbians in your congregations. I would, though, assure you that you don't find lesbians just among the single women of the church, nor, of course, are all single women lesbians. What may come as a bit of a surprise is that lesbians are to be found in significant numbers among heterosexually married women, women trapped by their commitment to families and to husbands, women who know deep in themselves that their most authentic love relationships have been and perhaps even now are with women.

Perhaps more important might be a recounting of the hundreds of lesbians I have met in the past year who have left the church. I could relate hair-raising stories of how the church attempted to dehumanize them, of how much pain they have suffered at its hands. I could tell you of the rage that erupts in some of them at the suggestion of anything Christian and of the tolerant laughter that springs from others at the mention of such devitalized concepts as "sin" or "salvation."

Or I could fall into the old trap of trying to define a lesbian by male standards, by the same philosophy that says, "All the lesbian needs is a good lay with a real man to make her normal." The male notion of the lesbian is the sexual one: she is a lesbian simply because she "has sex" with women. Nothing could be farther from the truth. But *if* we were talking in man-language about lesbianism, I'd want to point out that what lesbians and gay men do in bed is *technically* no different from what many of you do in bed with your wives or husbands (assuming that you have a healthy and vivid sexual relationship). The pain is that although heterosexual couples do "it" and marriage manuals even recommend "it" to buck up an otherwise tired and dull sexual life, still you give lip service to the notion that the "missionary position" is the only proper mode of sexual expression. You support a hypocritical morality that sanctions only the sex act that is potentially progenerative. By your silence on any other mode of sexual expression you continue to oppress gay people every minute of every day.

But the main thing I want to share with you is twofold.

First, I cannot separate the lesbian from the woman. This is not only because my oppression has been more as a woman than as a lesbian (though that of course is true), but also because to me being a lesbian is what really being a woman means. I like to think that the way politically conscious lesbians "are" in the world today is the way all women were before the tyranny of the patriarchy. To be a lesbian is to be identified not by men or by a society made by men but by me, by a woman. And the more I am identified by/for me, by/for my own experience, by/for my own values, the more a full woman I feel I become.

More and more woman-identified women are emerging everyday. More and more lesbians. It's not that more and more women are leaping into bed with each other. That may be your fantasy—certainly it is a common male fantasy—as to what lesbianism is all about. And indeed, my understanding is that astounding numbers of women are extending their love relationships with other women into sexual dimensions. But that's not the distinguishing characteristics of a lesbian. Lesbianism is a life-style, a mind-set, a body of experience. I would like to call any woman-identified woman a lesbian, and if she's really woman-identified, she'll feel good about being called a lesbian, whether or not she's had any sexual relationship with another woman.

The woman-identified women who are being reborn every day are those who are shaking off the chains forged by thousands of years of ecclesiastical propaganda. Shaking off their definition as male property, as male's helpmate, as the pure and empedestaled virtue-vessels that need chivalrous male protection. They are the unladylike women, the angry women, the ones who make you feel a little uneasy with their freedom of body, with the way they cross their legs or open their own car doors, or the way they look as though they'll give you a karate chop if you hassle them. They are the ones who reach a deep and threatening place inside every man's gut, the ones who can make your stomach turn over because they represent a truth that your own stomach has always secretly known. Particularly if you are a man, you both hate and admire their independence, their strength.

The women being reborn today (that's the real meaning of resurrection) are the ones marching for the rights to their own bodies at abortion demonstrations. Often they are women of witch-like appearance, women in jeans and boots who have laid away the girdles and garters that bound them into the profiteering system. They are women whose faces are honest, whose hair flies free, whose minds and bodies are growing supple and steady and sure in self-possession, whose love is growing deep and wide in the realities of newly discovered relationships with other women.

They don't need the church. The last thing they think about now is the church. They have within themselves what the church has claimed as its own and distorted so ironically for its own economic and psychological purposes these thousands of years.

Second, being a lesbian involves for me some growing political consciousness. That means I am committed to assessing institutions like the church, which, as far as women are concerned, takes the prize as the most insidiously oppressive institution in Western society. The matter of its influence needs no elaborating. Its insidiousness lies most obviously in the fact that it has made women (particularly white women) not only victims but murderers in a complex and exploitative economic system. One of the greatest marks of women's oppression is our conviction that we are not oppressed.

I look forward with great anticipation to the death of the church. The sooner it dies, the sooner we can go about the business of living the gospel. That living cannot take place in the church, and I suspect that most of us here have known that for a long time. But if we count on "renewal" or "reform" then we understand neither the depth of the church's crime nor the nature of the women's movement. If we count on "renewal" or "reform," then clearly we have not heard the voices of Third World peoples here and abroad.

Renewal and reform are not enough. Renewal and reform are more often sops, liberal cop-outs and tokenism in the face of real and harder tasks. For example, with gritted teeth some denominations offer to ordain women. They then expect me to rejoice in this, light bonfires on the hillside, and dance around the sacred flame. Far from rejoicing, I really feel sick, sick that woman energy shall now officially be made captive to the institutions, sick that in the very act of ordination a woman has separated herself from me and from others. She has played the church's game for good reason—in order to secure her survival. But in doing so, she hasn't challenged the church. She has only mounted another pedestal.

I am weary of the timid reassurances that "things are changing," or that "our congregation/pastor/district/seminary is different," or that you have to play the system's game to get into a power position so you can do some good. I mistrust with all my woman-heart the motive that keeps women committed to church renewal, i.e., "The church *needs* me." I am tired of hearing liberal churchpeople (both women and men) lay out transforming radical ideas in private and then collapse into meek submission in public when the chips are down. But I do understand why it happens: I know how important in this society it is to get a paycheck.

I long to hear voices *in public church gatherings* insisting not only upon the death of the institutional church but upon specific ways of carrying out that goal. In other words, I want to hear voices (so bold in private) insisting *in public* upon programs that affirm plural relationships, collective and communal living, same-sex love relationships, childhood sexuality, masturbating, and self-love. I want loud voices protesting sex-role socialization: that is, our practice of brainwashing people with outside plumbing to assume the role of strong-dominant-active-intelligent-conquering HE-MAN and those with inside plumbing to assume that of weak-submissive-receptive-dumb-conquered GIRL. Of course if such voices are heard, they are not likely to be heard again very often under the rafters of the institutional church. Such speakers have to be prepared to be ousted—and that, after all, may be the real point.

What is devastating and dehumanizing about the church is not its foundation of love, but the superstructure of patriarchal, theological claptrap that has been hoisted on that foundation. The superstructure shivers and quakes whenever the sanctity of the nuclear family or the traditional concepts of sexuality are called into question—and well it might shake, for it is these two concepts that are the bricks and mortar of the church.

The structure of the church (God over man, man over woman, father over family, clergy over laity, power over powerlessness) is vertical, hierarchical. The church's very identity depends on that hierarchy. This identity is dependent upon standards of success and failure, on authority, on competition.

It is dependent on who has power over whom. The idea is that God is at the top with power over all, and I as woman am at the bottom of the heap. Together with my children passivity is sanctified.

It will do no good to "renew" this church. If the gospel is to live, then vertical structure will have to be laid on its side— horizontalized—and that, to me, means the death of the institutional church.

Women who are being reborn these days do not want a man to step down from the pulpit so that a woman can step into it. They would do away with the pulpit altogether—do away with the physical setting apart of any person for purposes of "preaching" or "teaching."

Women of high consciousness do not want an equalization of the number of women and men on church councils. They would do away with councils themselves, with any body of people that is anything but voluntary and open to anyone concerned.

Women who are really getting it together don't want to be national presidents or bishops or pope. They don't want presidents, bishops, popes, and the like to exist at all, for the very definition of their office puts them above some and below others.

Woman-identified women don't want the Bible rewritten to talk about God-the-Mother or Jesus the Savioress. The women I have in mind believe that each person creates herself out of her own experience and that we must all work out in community our salvation from the repressive system we've grown up with.

Women who think of a revolution don't want just to have "ladies' Sunday" in the local congregation, where women run the show. They want to do away with the show altogether, because as it presently exists it is just that: a performance and not a participation. They do not want traditional worship, because that calls for craning their necks to look up or for bowing their heads in subjugation. They are only now learning what it means to look with love eyeball to eyeball with equals.

What can it mean to individuals in the church that they must begin to conduct the church's funeral, that they must themselves be the agents of the church's death? It must mean at least risks never taken before. It might mean, on an action level, throwing out the phallic pulpit that sets one person higher than and apart from another. Or it might mean tearing out puritanical pews and putting in comfortable chairs and pillows for being-with rather than being-under. Then the otherwise unused building can become a crash-pad or a refuge for transients—surely the church should be a refuge I use every hour of every week in the shelter and care of human beings.

It might be a good thing to use a generic "she" or "woman" or "woman-kind" in all our conversations for a decade or so instead of the masculine generic so men can begin to understand what it feels like to be made invisible.

You pastors can refuse to preach anymore, refuse to be the enlightened shepherds of a blind flock. You can also suggest some primitive Christianity in the form of pooled salaries and resources in your congregation—which would be divided according to need. All of this, of course, is with full knowledge that if you try any of it you're likely to be spewed out of the mouth of the church (ironically, because you are *not* lukewarm). Then perhaps you can come into the streets and ghettos of the secular world where the gospel is being discovered and lived.

But to make such changes—if you should succeed—is still to treat only the symptoms. We don't really get anywhere toward toppling the church structure until we articulate loud and clear some fundamental assumptions.

That traditional Christian teaching is anti-life; it is antithetical to any liberation ideology, its enfleshment, Christian practice, is not enfleshment at all but one of the Western world's most eloquent expressions of the fascist mind-set.

That traditional Christian concepts are the constructs of male
thinking and depend for their perpetuation on the myth of
male superiority.

That because the submission of women is absolutely essential to the church's functioning, the church has a vested
interest (economic and psychological) in perpetuating the
institutions that most oppress women: the nuclear family
and the sex-role socialization of children.

When we admit these things, then we can commit ourselves to
one of only two paths: either toppling the hierarchy completely
(which action would be the destruction of the church), or packing
up whatever shred of personal worth we've got left and leaving the
church entirely—hopefully in a hell-raising burst of glory that in
itself may educate other Christians.

So, as a woman, as a lesbian, I invite you not to attempt reform
of the church. I invite you either to destroy it or to desert it. Personal integrity allows no other alternatives.

Harvey Milk

The Hope Speech
(San Francisco, 1978)

Harvey Milk [1930–1978] was the first openly gay man to hold public office in California when he was elected to the San Francisco Board of Supervisors in 1977. Milk delivered the following speech, which would only later come to be known as "The Hope Speech," at the 1978 San Francisco Gay Freedom Day Parade. Harvey Milk was assassinated by former San Francisco Supervisor Dan White on November 27, 1978, just five months after giving this speech.

MY NAME is Harvey Milk and I'm here to recruit you.

I've been saying this one for years. It's a political joke. I can't help it—I've got to tell it. I've never been able to talk to this many political people before, so if I tell you nothing else you may be able to go home laughing a bit.

This ocean liner was going across the ocean and it sank. And there was one little piece of wood floating and three people swam to it and they realized only one person could hold on to it. So they had a little debate about which was the person. It so happened that the three people were the Pope, the President, and Mayor Daley. The Pope said he was titular head of one of the greatest religions of the world and he was spiritual adviser to many, many millions and he went on and pontificated and they thought it was a good

65

argument. Then the President said he was leader of the largest and most powerful nation of the world. What takes place in this country affects the whole world and they thought that was a good argument. And Mayor Daley said he was mayor of the backbone of the United States and what took place in Chicago affected the world, and what took place in the archdiocese of Chicago affected Catholicism. And they thought that was a good argument. So they did it the democratic way and voted. And Daley won, seven to two.

About six months ago, Anita Bryant in her speaking to God said that the drought in California was because of the gay people. On November 9, the day after I got elected, it started to rain. On the day I got sworn in, we walked to City Hall and it was kinda nice, and as soon as I said the word "I do," it started to rain again. It's been raining since then and the people of San Francisco figure the only way to stop it is to do a recall petition. That's the local joke.

So much for that. Why are we here? Why are gay people here? And what's happening? What's happening to me is the antithesis of what you read about in the papers and what you hear about on the radio. You hear about and read about this movement to the right. That we must band together and fight back this movement to the right. And I'm here to go ahead and say that what you hear and read is what they want you to think because it's not happening. The major media in this country has talked about the movement to the right so the legislators think that there is indeed a movement to the right and that the Congress and the legislators and the city councils will start to move to the right the way the major media want them. So they keep on talking about this move to the right.

So let's look at 1977 and see if there was indeed a move to the right. In 1977, gay people had their rights taken away from them in Miami. But you must remember that in the week before Miami and the week after that, the word homosexual or gay appeared in every single newspaper in this nation in articles both pro and con. In every radio station, in every TV station and every household. For the first time in the history of the world, everybody was talking about it, good or bad. Unless you have dialogue, unless you open the walls of dialogue, you can never reach to change people's opinion. In those two weeks, more good and bad, but more about the word homosexual and gay was written than probably in the history of mankind. Once you have dialogue starting, you know you can break down prejudice. In 1977 we saw a dialogue start. In 1977, we saw a gay person elected in San Francisco. In 1977 we saw the state of Mississippi decriminalize marijuana. In 1977, we saw the convention of conventions in Houston. And I want to know where the movement to the right is happening.

What that is, is a record of what happened last year. What we must do is make sure that 1978 continues the movement that is really happening that the media don't want you to know about. That is the movement to the left. It's up to CDC to put the pressures on Sacramento—but to break down the walls and the barriers so the movement to the left continues and progress continues in the nation. We have before us coming up several issues we must speak out on. Probably the most important issue outside the Briggs—which we will come to—but we do know what will take place this June. We know there's an issue on the ballot called Jarvis–Gann. We hear the taxpayers talk about it on both sides. But what you don't hear is that it's probably the most racist issue on the ballot in a long time. In the city and county of San Francisco, if it passes and we indeed have to lay off people, who will they be? The last in, and the first in, and who are the last in but the minorities? Jarvis–Gann is a racist issue. We must address that issue. We must not talk away from it. We must not allow them to talk about the money it's going to save, because look at who's going to save the money and who's going to get hurt.

We also have another issue that we've started in some of the north counties and I hope in some of the south counties it continues. In San Francisco elections we're asking—at least we hope to ask—that the U.S. government put pressure on the closing of the South African consulate. That must happen. There is a major difference between an embassy in Washington which is a diplomatic bureau and a consulate in major cities. A consulate is there for one reason only—to promote business, economic gains, tourism, investment. And every time you have business going to South Africa, you're promoting a regime that's offensive.

In the city of San Francisco, if every one of 51 percent of that city were to go to South Africa, they would be treated as second-class citizens. That is an offense to the people of San Francisco and I hope all my colleagues up there will take every step we can to close down that consulate and hope that people in other parts of the state follow us in that lead. The battles must be started some place and CDC is the greatest place to start the battles. I know we are pressed for time so I'm going to cover just one more little point. That is to understand why it is important that gay people run for office and that gay people get elected. I know there are many people in this room who are running for central committee who are gay. I encourage you. There's a major reason why. If my non-gay friends and supporters in this room understand it, they'll probably understand why I've run so often before I finally made it. Y'see right now, there's a controversy going on in this convention about the gay governor. Is he speaking out enough? Is he strong enough for gay rights? And there is controversy and for us to say it is not would be foolish. Some people are satisfied and some people are not.

You see there is a major difference—and it remains a vital difference—between a friend and a gay person, a friend in office and a gay person in office. Gay people have been slandered nationwide. We've been tarred and we've been brushed with the picture of pornography. In Dade County, we were accused of child molestation. It's not enough anymore just to have friends represent us. No matter how good that friend may be.

The black community made up its mind to that a long time ago. That the myths against blacks can only be dispelled by electing black leaders, so the black community could be judged by the leaders and not by the myths or black criminals. The Spanish community must not be judged by Latin criminals or myths. The Asian community must not be judged by Asian criminals or myths. The Italian community must not be judged by the mafia myths. And the time has come when the gay community must not be judged by our criminals and myths.

Like every other group, we must be judged by our leaders and by those who are themselves gay, those who are visible. For invisible, we remain in limbo—a myth, a person with no parents, no brothers, no sisters, no friends who are straight, no important positions in employment. A tenth of the nation supposedly composed of stereotypes and would-be seducers of children—and no offense meant to the stereotypes. But today, the black community is not judged by its friends, but by its black legislators and leaders. And we must give people the chance to judge us by our leaders and legislators. A gay person in office can set a tone, can command respect not only from the larger community, but from the young people in our own community who need both examples and hope.

The first gay people we elect must be strong. They must not be content to sit in the back of the bus. They must not be content to accept pablum. They must be above wheeling and dealing. They must be—for the good of all of us—independent, unbought. The anger and the frustrations that some of us feel is because we are misunderstood, and friends can't feel the anger and frustration. They can sense it in us, but they can't feel it. Because a friend has never gone through what is known as coming out. I will never forget what it was like coming out and having nobody to look up toward. I remember the lack of hope—and our friends can't fulfill it.

I can't forget the looks on faces of people who've lost hope. Be they gay, be they seniors, be they blacks looking for an almost-impossible job, be they Latins trying to explain their problems and aspirations in a tongue that's foreign to them. I personally will never forget that people are more important than buildings. I use the word "I" because I'm proud. I stand here tonight in front of my gay sisters, brothers and friends because I'm proud of you. I think it's time that we have many legislators who are gay and proud of that fact and do not have to remain in the closet. I think that a gay person, up-front, will not walk away from a responsibility and be afraid of being tossed out of office. After Dade County, I walked among the angry and the frustrated night after night and I looked at their faces. And in San Francisco, three days before Gay Pride Day, a person was killed just because he was gay. And that night, I walked among the sad and the frustrated at City Hall in San Francisco and later that night as they lit candles on Castro Street and stood in silence, reaching out for some symbolic thing that would give them hope. These were strong people, whose faces I knew from the shop, the streets, meetings and people who I never saw before but I knew. They were strong, but even they needed hope.

And the young gay people in the Altoona, Pennsylvanias, and the Richmond, Minnesotas, who are coming out and hear Anita Bryant on television and her story. The only thing they have to look forward to is hope. And you have to give them hope. Hope for a better world, hope for a better tomorrow, hope for a better place to come to if the pressures at home are too great. Hope that all will be all right. Without hope, not only gays, but the blacks, the seniors, the handicapped, the us'es, the us'es will give up. And if you help elect to the central committee and other offices, more gay people, that gives a green light to all who feel disenfranchised, a green light to move forward. It means hope to a nation that has given up, because if a gay person makes it, the doors are open to everyone.

So if there is a message I have to give, it is that I've found one overriding thing about my personal election, it's the fact that if a gay person can be elected, it's a green light. And you and you and you, you have to give people hope. Thank you very much.

Harry Hay

Unity and More in '84
(Boston, Massachusetts, 1984)

Harry Hay [1912–2002] is best known for his work founding the Matta-
chine Society, and as a prominent leader in the early gay rights movement.
This speech, in which Hay discusses the state of the gay rights movement
in the mid-eighties, was delivered at the Boston Gay Pride Day Rally.

IF ANY of you come to Los Angeles for the Olympics next month, some Gay person, taking you on a tour of gay Los Angeles, might drive you to the brow of a hill overlooking the east side of a quiet, silvery lake. On a windy November afternoon, 34 years ago, five politically radical Gay Brothers sat down together on that hill, under a Live Oak which is gone now, to contemplate the vision for a novel type of Gay organizing I was working on—I had conceived of developing "consciousness-raising raps" which we thought of simply as discussion groups in those years. And we began to dream of a Gay Family Collective which one day might stretch from sea to shining sea.

The five of us were committing ourselves to inventing a new Minority . . . quoting THE MATTACHINE MISSIONS & PURPOSES collectively written by five and then by seven of us as of April 1951, "paralleling the emerging cultures of our Fellow Minorities . . . the Negro, Mexican, and Jewish people." (Negro was the racially approved word then—Black came later.) Alike with Galatea and Pinocchio, the moment the New Minority was cut out, pasted together, and stood up on its teetery feet, it took off like a feather in the wind on a life of its own, inviting us to seek cracks and crevices in the heretofore impregnable walls of prejudice imprisoning us, through which our pent-up energies . . . now suddenly illuminated by political thought and direction . . . might at last begin to flow.

As spokesperson for that newly-invented but already impatient Minority, we five projected three immediate needs:

- to discover, or re-discover, who we Gay People were, where we had been over the millennia, and what we were for;
- to find ways and means of communicating our discoveries as to who we were, and what we were all about, to the Hetero Society surrounding us;
- to negotiate "free and equal" social and political spaces for our Minority—as a group—within that plurality of diverse Minority groups which comprises the American Community—wherein we could demonstrate what we were all about, wherein we could exercise and share the significant contributions we wished to make, the capacities for which we had been carrying and safeguarding down the many millennia of our refugee underground journeys.

Putting those right-brain feelings we had been secretly carrying within us—for many thousands of years—into left-brain words and phrases which could be written down and duplicated was one thing, to get any action started around them would prove to be quite something else.

When the committed five of us swelled to a sphere of influence of possible [*sic*] 5000 in the State of California by the Spring of 1953, even in the teeth of the McCarthy witch-hunt, we were in trouble. The majority—now middle class in outlook—swamped our radical perceptions and opted for the notion that we were the same as everybody else except in bed. With the advent of *Robert's Rules of Order,* the bright dreams of rediscovering ourselves died;

as the dreams died our sphere of influence plummeted from 5000 to 500. And though we laid little powder trains here and there, and began to win favorable decisions in court cases—including one in the United States Supreme Court—here and there; and occasionally we radicals were able to squirrel up chances to present positive Gay images on National Public Radio or on major TV here and there, the middle class cop-out remained largely the Movement's policy and outlook until Stonewall. The Stonewall eruption ignited the powder trains we radicals had been laying in many parts of the country. The combined explosions shattered the door-locks of the Hetero Society's closets and attics to reveal that we Gay and Lesbian folk were indeed everywhere. Gay lifestyles and Gay-positive ways of being ourselves suddenly became visible all over the place.

But the ways and means of communicating to the Hetero Society around us as to how we wished to be seen in terms of this new visibility, to be heard, were still not forthcoming. Such communications, which would have started to explain to them our startling new visibilities which—right from the first—were running athwart the long traditions of Hetero conformities, and threatening many a Hetero male's self-confidence, did not accompany our visibility presentations. The ways and means of communicating to the Hetero Society surrounding us about who we really were— and where we might be coming from or about how Great Mother Nature might have in mind for us to develop and contribute new dimensions of perceiving which Society desperately needs but for which discoveries Hetero Society was itself in no way equipped— all these powerful and even painful sharings which the Mattachine had projected as requiring to be our first priorities 20 years earlier, did not materialize any more after Stonewall than they had before Stonewall.

A month from now, over June 12 to June 13 in San Francisco, we may collectively face a national showdown instead of the merely state and local trouncing as of heretofore. Jerry Falwell, Phyllis Schlafly, the rabid Homophobic Catholic Priest Father Enrique Rueda, and the Reagan Administration in the persons of

Surgeon-General Koop, as well as the chairman of the National Endowment for the Humanities, and the Director of the Justice Department's Office of Juvenile Justice, are admittedly presenting a pro-Family conference at which THE THREAT OF HOMOSEXUALITY will be a major topic.

In the face of the long-announced plan of the Gay Movement Nationally to stage a giant march and rally on June 15th, to present to the Democratic Convention our determination to win first-class Citizenship;

- it has to be obvious that Falwell's single intention (as it is also of the massed forces of the New Right complete with official representation from the Reagan Administration) to taunt and goad the Gay Movement into dangerous inadvertencies of bitter and violent counter-actions.
- it has to be obvious that the massed forces of the New Right, together with the Reagan Administration, wish to embarrass the Gay Movement in the eyes of the world and so jeopardize their campaign to impress the Democratic Convention with the justice and the *human rightness* of their petitions;
- it has to be obvious that the New Right, through this "Pro-Family" conference, this FAMILY FORUM III being mounted by the Moral Majority Foundation and the Committee for the Survival of a Free Congress, is attempting to stampede the integrity of the Convention itself by shaming it into repudiating all those who would presumably undermine the sacred foundations of the Traditional American Family— Apple pie—Home and Mother!

Falwell, as a person and a citizen, is far too clever and intelligent to be in ignorance of who Gay people really are and of what the Gay Movement really consists. We are dealing with a hidden agenda here (and make no mistake!) a sinister and even dreadful "hidden agenda" in which the real victims are the American People themselves. The New Right, with Falwell as its principal spokesman, is deliberately and calculatingly laying the basis for the BIG LIE and creating, in consequence, the scapegoat classification

necessary to support it—exactly as did National Socialism, with
Hitler as its spokesperson, in Germany 44 years ago. The BIG LIE,
for Americans in 1984, is the Moral Majority version of the *Traditional American Family,* the family with the consciousness of Cotton
Mather, the family where the roles have retrogressed to the menial
servitudes for the women and children of families 100 years ago.
The American People must be informed that Falwell's Family
is the one in which Father is the autocrat solely responsible for,
and therefore in charge of, all of its affairs, where the differences
in the sexes have reverted to those laid out for all time in the Bible
"as they have been understood historically in the U.S."—to quote
the FAMILY PROTECTION ACT of the Hansen Bill HR#311, and the
Laxalt-Jepson Bill S#1378, of 1981-82.

And we Gay and Lesbian folks, in the Moral Majority's eyes,
are the prime threat to this noble Family Institution. It is by our
ever-increasing visibility not only in new applications of law and
social custom but indeed also in the Arts that we seduce and
recruit the children. But because we have never shared with our
friends and well-wishers in the grass-roots consensus of the American Community *our vision* as to who we are and what we might
really be about, that usually kindly-disposed American Consensus
has now no bottom line of informed opinion or shared experience
concerning us by which to fend off this barrage of evil and scur-
rilous deceit parading as religion and holy writ.

However, this time round, in this particular juncture of the
upcoming San Francisco convention, we may still have a legitimate way out. We Lesbians and Gays can point out, and rightly
so, that PRO-FAMILY III is but one segment of the National Community demanding audience of other segments of that same National
Community . . . it is not yet a United National Community
confronting us as a commonly-perceived *Scapegoat.* The Moral
Majority's irresponsible behavior should be reprehended by sober
and responsible heads from other segments of that same National
Community. I would propose that the combined forces of Gary
Hart, a Senator of the 97th Congress who studied and shelved
the FAMILY PROTECTION ACT, and of Jesse Jackson, a courageous

innovator in our National Religious community, together should proceed to expose and reveal the BIG LIE in the true measure of Falwell's Traditional American Family. I propose that Hart and Jackson reveal for all to see that the Moral Majority, to defend the authority of this American Family, are demanding through the FAMILY PROTECTION ACT—Federal law changes that would cut off all federal funds from any state or local agency who maintained shelters or provided assistance for battered women.

The MORAL MAJORITY, through the Family Protection Act, demand federal law changes so that child abuse would no longer be deemed to include corporal punishment when applied "reasonably" by a "responsible" parent or substitute, such substitutes being, among others, school teachers. They demand that all federal funds be cut off from any state or local agency who maintained shelters or provided assistance programs for child-victims of parental abuse or family abuse. Gary Hart and Jesse Jackson, as political leaders who seek to chart new paths for the American Community, are precisely the right spokespersons to examine whether Falwell's and Schlafly's and Reagan's Family, wherein women and children can be battered and abused without recourse are indeed the Family role models for a New American Consensus. Hart and Jackson can easily expose the wicked fraud of *this* Traditional American Family . . . and so stop this BIG LIE dead in its tracks while there is still time.

I propose that in the very beginning of our evaluative sharing circles we begin to catalog these differences as sharply and as precisely as we are able. For in the so doing we may simultaneously begin to discern a focus by which to appreciate the unexpected wealth and resources which the width and breadth of these visions— differences between the Lesbians and the Gays can afford us.

These are some of the ways, I think, that we might use to teach one another who we are and what we might really be about. Out of a true unity between the Lesbians and Gay men based upon a strong and mutual respect for each other's differences, we will be finally in a place to confront the necessity of demonstrating to the Hetero Community what we are really all about. When we begin to do this, incidently, and—here and there—manage to create a revelation whereby they suddenly comprehend who we are and how we have been contributing to their cultural and political well-being all these many millennia . . . and whereby they also catch wise to the suspicion that their laws and prejudices already are impeding us from making further contributions, we'll begin to see the Heteros moving to eliminate those repressive laws and customs *to their advantage* in order to keep our creative and inventive goodies flowing their way. And it is here—when they change the Laws not to our advantage but rather to their advantage—i.e., so that it conforms to the Consensus of the Whole—where our real security as a People resides.

So let us begin!

Sue Hyde

We Gather in Dubuque
(Dubuque, Iowa, April 30, 1988)

Sue Hyde is a prominent community organizer, writer, and speaker, best known for her work on the National Gay and Lesbian Task Force, where she serves as director of the annual Creating Change Conference. Hyde gave the following speech at the Second Annual Gay and Lesbian Pride March in Dubuque.

MY TRIP to Dubuque started me thinking about my own lesbian childhood and adolescence in a small town in Illinois. I grew up in Beardstown, Illinois, about 150 miles from where we stand today. I grew up in a town in which there were no black people, no Jewish people, and no openly lesbian and gay people, at least that I knew. Although, I am living testimony to the fact that we were there and still are, I'm sure.

The only time I ever saw black people was on the annual trip to St. Louis, Missouri to watch professional baseball games. I knew that the black people I saw were different from me. And in my child's mind, my white family, white friends, and white neighbors lived apart from these different-looking people because that was just the way the world was. Later I learned truths about the world: truths conveyed by these ugly words: racism, segregation and discrimination. Later I learned that my friendly, safe little white town had, through the 1930s and 1940s, posted signs at the city limits which read "Nigger, don't let the sun set on you here." Later I learned that the differentness of black people made them targets of white people's unaccountable suspicion and rage. But in my 11-year-old's mind, white people did not have black neighbors and that was just the way the world was. And that lie informed my thinking and shaped my consciousness.

I suspect many of us here today grew up with that same lie. And, as we discovered our sexualities, we knew we had been duped again. Duped into believing that our gay and lesbian sexuality necessarily sentenced us to a lifetime of unhappiness, proscribed by our shame and fear. We gather here in Dubuque to name those lies and to speak our own truths so that this community and this world will be forever changed.

We gather in Dubuque today so that none of us will ever feel afraid to walk this city's streets. Freedom of movement is such a basic right that we assume it for ourselves, especially if we are white and male. Thus, last Sept. 19, 30 lesbian and gay citizens took to these streets in a first ever Dubuque lesbian and gay pride march, only to be met by some 300 angry counter-demonstrators. The marchers were pelted with eggs while the police stood by and watched.

The march was cut short that day. But its organizers vowed to return this year because they would not simply bow down to the way Dubuque is. They did not agonize: they organized. And a wonderful thing happened. Ginny Lyons and Stacy Neldaughter, with their spark of courage, lit a fire of resistance and fueled a movement of gay men and lesbians to travel across the state, across the Midwest, and even across the country to stand with them today.

We have come to Dubuque to challenge it to be the best city it can be and to recognize and welcome its lesbian and gay citizens and to acknowledge their contributions to the quality of life here.

We challenge the Dubuque Human Relations Commission and the Dubuque City Council to amend the city's civil rights code to include sexual orientation. And if the events of last year's march are not evidence enough of the need for this, some people in this city have their eyes closed to reality. We challenge the city's police chief to open his mind to a proposal for sensitivity training for the members of his force.

And we challenge Mayor James Brady to realize that our sexuality is not simply a private matter, especially when he himself is quoted in the paper as saying "I wouldn't want to live next door to one." Mayor Brady, we want you to know that there is nothing private about your public declarations of bigotry and hate.

Mayor Brady and others no doubt feel uncomfortable about this demonstration. They no doubt feel unsettled by our challenge. They no doubt will breathe a sigh of relief when our buses and cars and trains pull out of town. But each man, woman and child in Dubuque has a responsibility to treat every other citizen with respect. And to the lesbian and gay citizens of Dubuque—the women and men who live, work and love here—Dubuque has a special responsibility to make this city safe for them, and to make last year's disgrace this year's triumph.

No more harassment. No more eggs or rocks or ugly words. No more governmental neglect and malevolence. No more fear. No more hate. No more silence. We choke on your hatred. We smother under your fear. We die of your red tape. And we cannot wait any longer to live.

With one voice, as one people, as a single wave inevitably crashes onto the shore, we say to you that our time for freedom has arrived. We promise to return to Dubuque each year until we no longer need to.

We invoke the spirits of Mahatma Gandhi, Fannie Lou Hamer, Martin Luther King and Barbara Deming, all of whom devoted their lives to freedom and justice. We call on them to guide us, walk with us, and join our one voice as we say:

We won't give up. We won't shut up. We won't go away.

And we will change this world.

Urvashi Vaid

Speech at the March on Washington
(Washington, D.C., April 25, 1993)

Urvashi Vaid [born 1958] is an American attorney, writer, and political activist of Indian descent, known for her decades of work promoting gay rights and social justice. She currently serves as the executive director of the Arcus Foundation, an organization dedicated to the promotion of human rights and conservation throughout the world. The following speech was delivered at the second March on Washington in support of gay and lesbian rights.

HELLO, LESBIAN and gay Americans. I am proud to stand before you as a lesbian today.

With hearts full of love and an abiding faith in justice, we have come to Washington to speak to America. We have come to speak the truth of our lives and silence the liars. We have come to challenge the cowardly Congress to end its paralysis and exercise moral leadership. We have come to defend our honor and win our equality.

But most of all we have come in peace and with courage to say, "America, this day marks the end from exile of the gay and lesbian people. We are banished no more. We wander the wilderness of despair no more. We are afraid no more. For on this day, with love in our hearts, we have come out. We have come out across

America to build a bridge of understanding, a bridge of progress, a bridge as solid as steel. A bridge to a land where no one suffers prejudice because of their sexual orientation, their race, their gender, their religion, or their human difference."

I have been asked by the March organizers to speak in five minutes about the Far Right. The Far Right, which threatens the construction of that bridge. The extreme Right which has targeted every one of you, and me, for extinction. The Supremacist Right which seeks to redefine the very meaning of democracy.

Language itself fails in this task, my friends, for to call our opponents "the Right," states a profound untruth. They are wrong. They are wrong morally, they are wrong spiritually, and they are wrong politically.

The Christian supremacists are wrong spiritually when they demonize us. They are wrong when they reduce the complexity and beauty of our spirit into a freak show.

They are wrong spiritually, because, if we are the untouchables of America—if we are the untouchables—then we are, as Mahatma Gandhi said, children of God. And as God's children we know that the Gods of our understanding, the Gods of goodness and love and righteousness, march right here with us today.

The supremacists who lead the anti-gay crusade are wrong morally. They are wrong because justice is moral, and prejudice is evil; because truth is moral and the lie of the closet is the real sin; because the claim of morality is a subtle sort of subterfuge, a stratagem which hides the real aim which is much more secular.

Christian supremacist leaders like Bill Bennett and Pat Robertson, Lou Sheldon and Pat Buchanan, supremacists like Phyllis Schlafly, Ralph Reed, Bill Kristol, R. J. Rushdoony—these supremacists don't care about morality, they care about power. They care about social control. And their goal, my friends, is the reconstruction of American Democracy into American Theocracy.

We who are gathered here today must prove the religious Right wrong politically. And we can do it. That is our challenge.

You know they have made us into the communists of the

nineties. They say they have declared cultural war against us. It's war all right. It's a war about values.

On one side are the values that everyone here stands for. Do you know what those values are? Traditional American values of democracy and pluralism. On the other side are those who want to turn the Christian church into government, those whose value is monotheism.

We believe in democracy, in many voices co-existing in peace, and people of all faiths living together in harmony under a common civil framework known as the United States Constitution.

Our opponents believe in monotheism. One way—theirs. One God—theirs. One law—the Old Testament. One nation supreme—the Christian Right one. Let's name it. Democracy battles theism in Oregon, in Colorado, in Florida, in Maine, in Arizona, in Michigan, in Ohio, in Idaho, in Washington, in Montana, in every state where my brothers and sisters are leading the fight to oppose the Right and to defend the United States Constitution.

We won the anti-gay measure in Oregon, but today 33 counties—33 counties and municipalities face local versions of that ordinance today.

The fight has just begun. We lost the big fight in Colorado, but, thanks to the hard work of all the people of Colorado, the Boycott Colorado movement is working and we are strong. And we are going to win our freedom there eventually.

To defeat the Right politically, my friends, is our challenge when we leave this March.

How can we do it? We've got to March from Washington into action at home.

I challenge everyone of you, straight or gay, who can hear my voice, to join the national gay and lesbian movement. I challenge you to join the National Gay and Lesbian Task Force to fight the Right. We have got to match the power of the Christian supremacists, member for member, vote for vote, dollar for dollar.

I challenge each of you, not just buy a T-shirt, but [also] get involved in your movement. Get involved! Volunteer! Volunteer!

Every local organization in this country needs you. Every clinic, every hotline, every youth program needs you, needs your time and your love.

And I also challenge our straight liberal allies, liberals and libertarians, independent and conservative, republican or radical. I challenge and invite you to open your eyes and embrace us without fear.

The gay rights movement is not a party. It is not [a] lifestyle. It is not a hairstyle. It is not a fad or a fringe or a sickness. It is not about sin or salvation.

The gay rights movement is an integral part of the American promise of freedom.

We, you and I, each of us, we are the descendents of a proud tradition of people asserting our dignity.

It is fitting that the Holocaust Museum was dedicated the same weekend as this March, for not only were gay people persecuted by the Nazi state, but [also] gay people are indebted to the struggle of the Jewish people against bigotry and intolerance.

It is fitting that the NAACP marches with us, that feminist leaders march with us, because we are indebted to those movements.

When all of us who believe in freedom and diversity see this gathering, we see beauty and power.

When our enemies see this gathering, they see the millennium, the end of the world.

Perhaps the Right is right about something. We stand for the end of the world as we know it. We call for the end of racism and sexism and bigotry as we know it. We call for the end of violence and discrimination and homophobia as we know it. We call for the end of sexism as we know it.

We stand for freedom as we have yet to know it. And we will not be denied.

Jim Kepner

*Why Can't We All Get Together,
and What Do We Have in Common?*
(April 28, 1997)

*Jim Kepner [1923–1997] was an American journalist, historian, and gay
rights activist, best known for the pioneering journalistic and archival work
he did for* One *Magazine, the first U.S. pro-gay publication. Kepner
delivered this speech, based on the 1985 monograph of the same name,
just a few months before his death.*

GAYS AND Lesbians often agonize because our movement doesn't
move directly toward that ultimate goal they're sure all of us
want. But—is our goal clearly agreed on? It is not, and nothing
has so hampered our movement as our failure to understand our
legitimate differences regarding goals. We'll continue to rip our
movement apart unless we clearly understand this diversity and its
consequences. Our movement's history suggests that our diversity
is more than just something to be tolerated.

That history shows how religious Gays and atheists, conservatives and radicals, feminists, radical faeries, transsexuals, boy lovers,
minorities and PWAs have built up the debate about our movement goals. Not until the late '60s did many activists admit that
such differences are legitimate, and begin to see that our diversity
has some advantages. Note that I generally use the terms Gay,

Homophile and homosexual as Gay men and women did then, to include both (or all) genders.

I don't like lazy speeches that take an hour to say what can be said in a few sentences, so I'm going to cover a lot of ground—and jump around a bit. I hope you'll all jump when I jump.

I knew I was different by age four, but had a long search to define that difference and to relate my perceptions to the group I would seek out to share with. I define myself differently today from when, from age 12 to 17, I planned to be a Presbyterian missionary to the Congo. I came out in San Francisco in 1943, but took side trips through pacifism, militant atheism, science fiction fandom and the Communist Party before I found my way to our fledgling Gay movement in 1953. These "side trip" identities with other groups and causes helped shape my perceptions on who we are and what we might become. Memories of my former beliefs, and the emotional residue each has left in my gut, help me appreciate the diverse ways in which other Gays and Lesbians define ourselves and our goals.

ULRICHS AND HIRSCHFELD

Most founders of the first stable U.S. Gay organization didn't know in 1950–51 that our movement was born in Germany in 1896, after 30 years of pioneering by Karl Ulrichs—and a few earlier persons who'd argued in our behalf. Many of our goals were first defined in the pre-Nazi German movement for homosexual rights.

Karl Heinrich Ulrichs responded to an immediate threat: the several independent German states were being swallowed by Prussia, which had a severe anti-homosexual law. Ulrichs, a civil servant in Hanover, opposed the unification which would criminalize all German homosexuals. He informed his relatives of his nature, and of his plan for a public campaign for education and justice, then appealed for justice for what he called "Urnings," at a Jurists' conference, where he was shouted down. He said that having gone public, he and his cause could never turn back.

He took the term Urning from Plato's *Symposium*, mentioning Uranus as God of same-sex lovers. Ulrichs' first goal was to work out a theory as to Who are we? How do we get this way? And does nature have a reason for so regularly producing us?—an idea revived by Sociobiologists today. He was a prophet, but no organizer. The German movement got its real start the year after he died.

The first group was Der Eigene (community of the special), founded by Adolf Brand, Benedict Friedlander and publisher Max Spohr. Their goal was to build a separate and idealized male Gay culture, on the old Greek model. A radical German women's movement also started that year, and a hippie-like back-to-nature youth movement, rejecting bourgeois values and emphasizing erotic friendship. Socialism, spiritualism and health fads also blossomed until the Nazi takeover.

In 1897, the Der Eigene leaders joined Dr. Magnus Hirschfeld to form the Scientific-Humanitarian Committee, which Hirschfeld led. SHC goals were scientific research to show that the "intermediate sex" (which Hirschfeld compared to being crippled) was inborn, and a campaign to solicit influential people to reform the law, arguing that homosexuals can't help being the way they are, and that the law encouraged blackmail. Friedlander and some women's leaders scorned the comparison to cripples, whom society might tolerate, but never accept as equals. They also spurned Hirschfeld's and Ulrichs' view that male homosexuals were by nature womanish.

Five thousand illustrious persons ultimately signed the law reform petition: Einstein, Hermann Hesse, Socialist leaders August Bebel and Karl Kautsky, Freud, Krafft-Ebing, Martin Buber, Karl Jaspers, George Grosz, Heinrich and Thomas Mann, Carl Maria von Weber, Stefan Zweig, Gerhardt Hauptman, Rainer Maria Rilke, Arthur Schnitzler, even Berlin's police chief and the Prussian and Federal Ministers of Justice—but no publicly identified homosexuals.

In 1898 the issue came before Germany's Reichstag—supported only by minority Social Democrats. In 1907 a right-wing newspaper attack on Prince Eulenburg and other Gay intimates of the Emperor killed the reform, and hurt the movement, as Hirschfeld testified against the defendants as a police witness. Hirschfeld, frustrated by the failure of influential Gays to help the cause, had discussed the controversial strategy revived by some AIDS activists recently—of forcing such persons out of the closet.

The reform bill was diverted in 1914 by World War I, and in 1923 by runaway inflation. It passed the Reichstag's Criminal Justice Committee but not the whole Reichstag—just before Hitler's takeover signaled the quick, total destruction of the German gay community.

Gay groups had diversified greatly. The law hadn't changed but police pressure had relaxed, so before the Nazi takeover, there were Gay and Lesbian cultural, pen pals, health, political, religious and social groups. Novelist Sinclair Lewis, in *Dodsworth,* described Gay neighborhoods in major German cities patrolled by friendly policemen. Hirschfeld, emphasizing education, published his thick *Yearbook for Intermediate Sexual Types* and build a massive library and school in Berlin, which the Nazis burned. With actor Conrad Veidt, he starred in the first Gay rights film, *Different From the Others,* and collected massive research to prove that homosexuality was inborn and that homosexuals, though effeminate, were fine citizens, even fine soldiers in World War I. He thought this information would end discrimination. Just when Hirschfeld and others thought they stood on the brink of victory, the holocaust swept them away. Untold thousands were worked to death in concentration camps. The Nazis saw Hirschfeld—Jew, homosexual, socialist and feminist—as their ultimate enemy.

Homophile leader Kurt Hiller had said that homosexuals must free themselves, not wait for others to do it. He was sent to a concentration camp, ransomed out, taught in England during the war, and came back to lead the German law reform campaign to success in 1968–69.

OTHER COUNTRIES

Similar groups were started in other countries. Dutch and Czech SHC groups started in 1911, the Dutch interrupted only by World War II's Nazi occupation. The COC, now called the Dutch

Society for Integration of Homosexuals, provided a safe meeting place and worked to lower age-of-consent laws. Most European groups assumed that homosexuals were middle or upper class, who sought boys or lower class men as partners.

Edward Carpenter, George Ives, Havelock and Edith Ellis, A.E. [and] Laurence Housman, Radclyffe Hall and others tried starting an English movement during the fearful years after Oscar Wilde's trial—aiming mainly at sex education. England's real movement came only in 1970 after massive witchhunts and 16 years debate on the Wolfenden law reform proposals. The Homosexual Law Reform Society during the 1950s and 60s had argued that homosexuals couldn't help being that way, and ought not be imprisoned—implying that homosexuals would gratefully become invisible once the law changed! Anglican, Catholic and British Medical Association reports supported this. Only the Quaker Report said that homosexuals were potentially as moral as heterosexuals.

A Zurich woman, Mammina, started the Swiss Friendship Bund in 1932 to provide social outlets, and work modestly on law reform. The name became Der Kreis or The Circle in 1943, after she handed the group over to prominent actor Karl Meier, a.k.a. Rolf. The only magazine and club to survive through World War II, Der Kreis added French and English sections during the fifties. With its Oktoberfests and other social activities, it was [an] international center for a select circle of Gay men, many of them American.

There was a small movement among intellectuals in pre-Communist Russia. Leo Tolstoy, a guiltily repressed homosexual, castigated Gay rights advocates in his 1899 novel *Resurrection,* but he signed Hirschfeld's petition. By 1905, Gays like poet Mikhail Kuzmin had produced a small body of Gay advocacy literature. The Bolsheviks removed Czarist anti-homosexual laws, and Gays became briefly more open. Lenin and Trotsky stayed homophobic, but initially viewed the traditional family as a bulwark of reaction. Most open Lesbian and Gay poets hailed the Revolution, but most of them soon came under house arrest.

Kuzmin issued his Gayest work after 1918—but in Amsterdam, not Russia. Some like the great poet Anna Akhmatova stood by their friends, until each was sent to Siberia. To survive, she had to publish fawning lines about Stalin.

At World League Congresses for Sexual Reform led by Hirschfeld from 1921 until 1930, Russian Health Minister Grigorii Batkis called the USSR a model of homosexual freedom, until he was silenced. The Soviets briefly promised a Gay homeland, in the far reaches of Siberia near Birobijan, the forgotten Jewish "homeland." The communists soon reverted to hetero conformity and ended talk of sex liberation. Gays were branded a sign of bourgeois decadence. Communists blamed fascism on homosexual excess, while the Nazis blamed us for the decadence of democracy.

Around 1913, anarchist Emma Goldman and Edith Ellis each lectured on homosexual rights to large responsive American crowds, according to contemporary press reports, and birth control advocate Margaret Sanger reportedly tried to set up some sort of organization. Hirschfeld toured the U.S. later, his talks enthusiastically reported for the Hearst press by pro-German Gay writer George Sylvester Viereck.

Lesbians, prominent in several artistic and literary circles, such as that around Margaret Fuller in early 19th century Boston, Charlotte Cushman later in Rome and Margaret Anderson in Chicago about 1913, seemed less likely than men to organize politically—except in the nineteenth-century abolitionist, prohibition and women's rights movements, where women-loving-women played leading roles but never *publicly* raised Lesbian issues. Few even defined themselves that way. They focused on freeing women from the worst tyrannies of marriage, endless childbearing and alcoholism, while opening to women social roles previously reserved for men.

Women fought to be able to attend and teach school, serve as nurses or foreign missionaries, dress more comfortably, build settlement houses to educate and assist immigrants, crusade for child labor laws, sanitation, etc., but most affectional relations were hidden behind "convenient" hetero marriages, or "Boston marriages" which were presumed to be romantic but sexless. The woman artists and writers who wanted to openly flout heterosexual expectations either moved to Europe or disguised themselves as men.

GERBER AND FRIENDS

Bavarian-born Henry Gerber, forerunner of America's movement, served in the U.S. World War I army in the Rhineland, discovering the thriving Gay movement there. Back in Chicago in 1924 he recruited eight ordinary guys for his Society for Human Rights, though he tried to win support from such leading sex reformers as Margaret Sanger. His group was all arrested and undistributed copies of their paper Friendship and Freedom were seized (two copies were recorded in European Gay periodicals.) After two trials, Gerber returned to the army, ran Contacts, a pen-pals club, for ten years from New York, and in '34 wrote for *Chanticleer*, a mimeographed atheist publication in which at least half the space went to Gay concerns—the earliest U.S. periodical of which copies exist. When Gerber folded Contacts in 1939, member Monwell Boyfrank pestered him to start some group through which like-minded men could meet. For some, that remains the primary goal of our movement. Gerber, Frank McCourt and Boyfrank corresponded for years, arguing how to organize and to what purpose. Their sharply differing views on the nature of homosexuality and of society left little room for them to agree on goals or tactics.

They hoped to educate opinion-makers about human sexuality, assuming that problems will vanish when people are informed of the truth. Gerber felt there always had been homosexuals and heteros, with undecided fools making things dangerous; yet he always cruised straight-looking servicemen. Convinced that religious superstition shackled sexuality, he advocated atheist propaganda as a prerequisite to homosexual freedom.

Boyfrank assumed that most men were drawn toward other men or boys, unless snared into providing for women's domestic needs. He sought sex with masculine-type men, but also argued to fathers (successfully, even in small towns) that their sons *need* a kindly older gent to provide the considerate love and guidance which fathers rarely have time for. He was proud when his boys grew up hetero. His atheism was milder than Gerber's. He saw marriage as the enemy. Later, recognizing the family's financial advantages, he urged men to form Federated Families, to save their property from relatives' clutches. (His own property went to his sister.)

McCourt held prayer meetings in a large Riverside Drive house during World War II for Gay soldiers about to be shipped over the submarine-infested Atlantic, Gerber raged at this arrant pandering to superstition. But it had to be comforting to Gay servicemen who weren't getting family support as they headed to the war many would not return from. McCourt studied Gay history and literature and worked to build circles of Gay friends with shared interests. All three viewed women as the source of sexual repression.

In 1944, after homophobic press coverage of a murder case, they started answering press slurs as the *Society Skirting Sexual Superstition*, a name they used only among themselves. Their over-long letters were often printed. Gerber's *In Defense of Homosexuality* was one of the first articles I found in 1942—in a freethinking magazine.

In Los Angeles, Edith Eyde, whom I'd known earlier, typed out her carbon-copy magazine *Vice-Versa–America's Gayest Magazine* in 1947–48, to inform Gay women about the subject. She hand-delivered them, mostly in a Lesbian bar, for fear of postal snoops who often seized or opened mail then. Two women readers later became editors of *ONE Magazine*. Edith later sang campy Gay folksongs at bars—as she did in the film *Before Stonewall*.

THE EARLY MATTACHINE

In Los Angeles' Pershing Square in 1930, a friend of Gerber's told young Harry Hay about the Society for Human Rights, inspiring Hay to imitation—even though the friend thought Gerber was a damned fool for trying to organize. But to start a group, you need at least one other person, and it took Hay 20 years to find that other—the later famed fashion designer Rudy Gernreich. Hay had gained valuable organizing experience in the Communist Party, plus unique views on the nature of homosexuality from his study of the musical expressions of peasant religions, in which he searched for Gay influences. Having discovered the American Indian Berdache, Hay followed Edward Carpenter's view that in tribal and medieval societies, we had been outsiders with special roles, and if we today seek assimilation, we sell our birthright for a mess of hetero pottage. He hoped to form underground mystic guilds, to reawaken ourselves to who we are and what we are for. In late 1950, he met three more men who shared his dream of Gays working openly in a socialist-led united front.

He showed a prospectus he'd drawn up earlier to Bob Hull, a student in his Social History of Music class. Bob brought his friends Chuck Rowland and Dale Jennings to Hay's Silverlake house. Chuck, a former American Veterans Committee Midwest organizer, supposedly ran up the hill waving the prospectus, saying, "I could have written this myself! When do we start?" (Chuck later denied that story.)

The fear-ridden society they faced was *very* different from that we live in today. People were being hounded, even arrested, for being different in any significant way. "Perverts" and subversives were considered largely the same—both threats to everything America stood for. Committed to making a socialist revolution, Hay and his new friends had to figure out how to make Gays part of that.

They began seeking consensus on how to create a movement *where none had seemed possible,* arguing every idea to agreement, lest they risk setbacks. They were groping in the dark, exchanging what little they knew about homosexuality before they could even think of social action. Two young motorcyclists joined five months later, brought in friends, such as photographer Ruth Bernhard, and chose the name Mattachine—from eleventh-century guilds of wandering actors Hay had described in his class.

They were painfully aware that America was in a dangerous, witch-hunting mood, and that Gays were a prime target. Hay's music class had unwittingly involved a search for Gay roots and roles. Communists had devoted attention to the minority question, so Hay proposed the radical notion that homosexuals were an oppressed minority, needing to build a sense of community. Most new members wildly resisted this idea, wanting only to be like-everyone-else.

Then Dale Jennings was charged with propositioning a vice cop. Since Gays and other minorities were angry about entrapment, they launched a Committee to Outlaw Entrapment, to raise defense funds and to hold public discussion groups, from which they could hunt for promising recruits. They soon drew crowds of 20 to 150 Gay men and a few Lesbians to weekly groups all over town, with topics very few Gays had ever before felt free to discuss in public:

Should I tell my parents, or my boss?
Can a Gay person still be religious?
Do we need a Gay ethics for special conditions in our lives?
Do we have a group purpose, a special way of serving society?
How can I meet nice responsible friends?
Why aren't there more women here?
Are swishes and bulldykes the cause of prejudice against us?

Few of the new recruits shared the founders' vision. Most of them saw homosexuality as just a sexual habit. They wanted nothing to do with other minorities, or with communists. In early '53, just as Mattachine reached San Diego, northern California and Chicago, with inquiries coming in from all over, Chuck Rowland and others, realizing the creakiness of the old lodge-like structure, called a constitutional convention to devise new structures. 100 [One hundred] of us, hot with optimism, certain that we were going to win our battle against bias soon, met at a Universalist church in Los Angeles. Few of us in those two weekends understood the bitter issues which ripped us apart. While we voted on dozens of confused proposals for a new organizational structure, the conservative-conformist newcomers generally routed the founders.

Anything remotely radical-sounding was knocked out, such as a Statement of Purpose clause: ". . . we hold it necessary that a highly ethical homosexual culture be integrated into society." The new leaders saw this as viciously communistic—I never understood how. One insurgent threatened to report us all to the FBI (saying that he'd already turned in hundreds of traitors.) The resulting constitution proved extremely contradictory, unstable and incomplete.

Optimism vanished and membership declined, though new chapters began in time in New York, Detroit and Denver. The Los Angeles council soon folded and headquarters moved to San Francisco. But there were also gains. The secretiveness was gone. *Mattachine Review*, several local newsletters and *Dorian Book Quarterly* along with *ONE Magazine,* brought an increasingly positive message to many isolated Gays. The most creative Mattachine chapter and newsletter was Denver's. Their 1959 national convention was our first professional-type event, the first to get fair, daily newspaper coverage.

ONE INCORPORATED

The idea for a magazine, called *ONE,* came up at a Mattachine discussion group, but the magazine committee quickly chose to be independent. Too feisty for most timid Mattachinos, *ONE* soon began to balance male and female contents. The women of *ONE* felt that women had a different sensitivity, but didn't yet envision "women's issues" as such. Most staffers felt *ONE* Incorporated existed *only* to produce a magazine "dealing with homosexuality from the scientific, historical and critical point of view," but business manager Dorr Legg had written in broader purposes ("to sponsor educational programs, lectures and concerts for the benefit of social variants and promote among the general public an interest, knowledge and understanding of the problems of variation . . . to sponsor research and promote integration . . ."

etc.) He saw it as *ONE*'s goal to create all the social service, cultural and educational institutions necessary for a well-rounded community. ·

Legg as a youth had seemed alone in looking for a community, not just a lay or a lover. He chose Los Angeles as the place to share life with a black lover—not easy then. Before joining Mattachine, he'd helped launch the short-lived interracial club, Knights of the Clocks. He exercised iron control over *ONE* Incorporated until his death in late 1994.

By early 1956, though we meant to concentrate on the magazine, counselees were coming to *ONE* desperate to escape the Hell they felt St. Paul had condemned them to. Ann Carrol Reid and I proposed kicking off a series of Sunday morning events, where ex-ministers or metaphysicians who were part of our circle could do whatever seemed appropriate to them: pray, preach, hold séances, hear confessions, meditate or lead singalongs. Chuck Rowland, head of our promotions committee, broke away and organized the Church of One Brotherhood. It grew steadily for a year, despite our angry scorn, and collapsed suddenly. They *did* help Gays suffering religious guilt, and ambitiously proposed to start a retirement home, a university, a hospital, etc., "as soon as they'd raised $100." What they tried was brought off successfully a dozen years later by Troy Perry. Several Gay Orthodox clergy branching out from the late Bishop Mikhail Itkin, claim descent from a reported 1945 Gay church in Atlanta.

In '56 we at *ONE* organized America's first Gay studies, surveying the academic fields of biology, anthropology, sociology, history, literature, religion, law and philosophy, asking what each could contribute to understanding how Gays fit into the nature of things. In 1958, I produced *ONE Institute Quarterly of Homophile Studies,* the first U.S. Gay scholarly journal. Issue #8, based on court cases defending the Right of Association in Gay bars, was widely used as a text in British law schools.

Don Slater, *ONE*'s chief editor and librarian after 1957, was a cantankerous individualist, denying that the state has a right to exist, much less to curb our behavior in any way. His sharp, campy style fit well with that of art editor Eve Elloree.

MY COMING OUT

From age four I was looking for a special friend, the brother I never had—in place of the marriage everybody said lay in wait. Not effeminate, I was uncomfortable with what a boy was supposed to be, and felt a common bond with tomboys. At 19, I first heard the word *homosexual*, loathsomely defined. With unusual luck, I found relevant books, which were rare and mostly awful then. I started the collection which ultimately grew into the International Gay and Lesbian Archives. It took me a year to find the Gay crowd, but because of a burst of police pressure, and because Gays expected one another to act effeminate, I later retreated back to the closet.

In science-fiction fandom, my closeted Gayness caused a minor scandal. From the radical movement, I was expelled in 1948 for being Gay. After several attempts to convince friends to join me in starting a Gay magazine or organization, I joined Mattachine in 1953 and *ONE* a bit later, helping edit *ONE Magazine* and other *ONE* publications through 1960. I helped start *ONE*'s classes, teaching Gay studies off and on since then in several cities.

At inter-group panels at annual meetings of *ONE*, Mattachine and the Lesbian Daughters of Bilitis during the late fifties, I likened the latter two to the cautious National Urban League, which sought quiet ways to up-grade Black social status. I compared *ONE* to the militant National Association for the Advancement of Colored People. Mattachine aimed to convince opinion makers that we were just like everyone else, so *they* would stop persecuting us. One Mattachine officer said their goal was to help cure us all. DOB aimed to provide nicer Lesbian meeting places than bars, urged members to avoid dress or behavior which might inflame bias, later argued that we must recognize that we are sick before society can respect us. *ONE* urged Gays to respect and understand themselves, to build the communal strength needed to win our rights. We looked for the social roots of prejudice, seeking tools to counter it.

In January '61, *ONE* planned a Constitutional Convention to write a *Homosexual Bill of Rights*. We mailed a questionnaire to subscribers. Dorr Legg and I agreed that some rights are general and some conditional. I'd hoped to analyze what Gays wanted. But Dorr, who despised the term Gay, composed a questionnaire whose answers couldn't be interpreted clearly or tabulated, and that asked irrelevantly (I felt) "what kind of sex acts do you prefer?" By conference time, I had left *ONE* for a complex set of reasons, and the DOB came down angrily opposed to even *thinking* about claiming any "special rights." The "Constitutional Convention" was a disaster.

After leaving *ONE,* I spent six years at cab driving and two at junior college, finding time to consider some general questions:

People often asked, "Why did Gays take so long to organize?" I recalled responses I'd had earlier when asking others to join me in organizing. Most Gays felt homosexuality was a sickness, a sin or both. Either way, organizing seemed inappropriate. Some longed for the conditions of ancient Greece, but without time machines, had no idea how to get back to that blessed state. Very few saw our problems as political, i.e., amenable to organizing, and most felt that while other social problems might be helped, society will always hate us. A few saw a need for organizing, but were fearful and unlikely to agree on a specific clear course. It was virtually a miracle that people came together for the original Mattachine as well as for the original DOB who could agree on the need to do something, and on what to do. That agreement was rather short-lived in both cases.

MID-SIXTIES GROUPS

In the early sixties, old groups stagnated and new ones brought new goals and strategies. After TV game shows were rocked in 1960 by *payola* scandals, the long-time habit of cops taking pay-offs in Gay bars backfired. San Francisco cops and state

Alcoholic Beverage Control agents busted each other for taking protection money. After nearly every Gay bar in town was closed and reopened, bar owners formed the Tavern Guild, a mutual defense league which launched a revolution beyond their hopes.

They began doing community-building, with appeals to patrons, social outings and voter registration. Then several S.F. Mattachine members, tired of their volunteer time being used for one officer's private business, walked out. In '64 a second walkout produced SIR, the Society for Individual Rights. SIR was creative and aggressive, with jargonless practical programs to cultivate genuine Gay community consciousness. They built special interest groups, registered voters, helped elect candidates to public office, staged dances, plays and picnics, worked with the Tavern Guild and helped launch the Council on Religion and the Homosexual. They studied community-organizing tactics (how to reach the corridors of power and influence those people who can move things) and helped create a National Conference of Homophile Organizations, or NACHO, aiming to coordinate U.S. and Canadian groups.

A *Hollywood Citizen-News* campaign to "drive 'Sex Deviates' out of town" created a flurry of new Los Angeles activity. The campaign, conceived ironically as a newspaper sales gimmick by a Gay staffer, eventually put the daily paper out of business—our first successful boycott.

PRIDE was a 1966 Los Angeles attempt to imitate SIR— but aside from one fine street protest against police brutality, and launching the newsletter which became *The Advocate*, PRIDE was torn apart by contrary goals and tactics—S.D.S.–like militancy competing with respectabilism [sic] and toadying to cure-peddlers.

Vanguard was started on San Francisco streets in 1966 by hustlers, some as young as 11, using Anglo-Saxon language, radical slogans and psychedelic art like later Gay Liberation Fronts. Until then, all NACHO groups, on strong legal advice, had refused to deal with minors, but these angry minors demanded we deal with them. We did.

An East Coast coalition led by Dr. Frank Kameny, Barbara Gittings and Jack Nichols, began picketing the White House and Independence Hall annually to demand equal justice. Nichols had called for rejecting the negative, Uncle Tom, attitudes many movement leaders had, and had approached Churchmen to deal with the subject. Dick Leitsch and Craig Rodwell held sip-ins at bars, protesting state regulations that bars can't serve known homosexuals. The DOB turned to general women's issues after 1970, objecting to the homophile movement's focus on men's arrests for public sex (though that was not an exclusively male problem.) A few Gays began criticizing some homophile groups' ties to cure-peddling shrinks.

Dr. Franklin Kameny of Washington planted Mattachine clone groups from New England to the Niagara Frontier. He insisted that we had no time for social activities, education and social service: "Until we get the law off our backs, we can't take time to pick up the flotsam and jetsam of a rotten society." Yet he was often charitable. He, Nichols and Gittings implacably fought military and civil service discrimination cases. Gittings later worked to get better images of Gays and Lesbians in libraries.

Not all Gays approached military counseling the same way: some used it to protect the right of privacy, some to oppose the war in Vietnam. Some began telling draft boards that they were Gay, whether they were or not. In some cities, Gays started VD clinics to halt the disease's spread. Others felt that VD couldn't be a special problem for us since Gays-are-just-like-everyone-else, and besides, they argued, VD tests served only to give police our names. These arguments resurfaced at higher pitch early in the AIDS crisis 20 years later.

Craig Rodwell, founder of the pioneering Oscar Wilde Memorial Bookstore, Randy Wicker and Bob Martin of Columbia University's Student Homophile League (a first), became militant young Turks on the east coast, upsetting the prissy conservative leaders. In San Francisco, young radicals attacked SIR and took the Black Panthers as models—Constantine Berlandt, who'd come

out while editing UC Berkeley's *Daily Californian*; ABC reporter
Leo Lawrence, radicalized when cops gassed him at Chicago's
1968 Democratic Convention; Vanguard veterans and the unstable Rev. Ray Broshears.

NACHO's founders in Kansas City and in San Francisco in
1966 tried to adjudicate between two factions claiming to represent *ONE*. Insurgent Don Slater (who'd moved everything of
value from *ONE*'s office in May '65) insisted that all homosex acts
are perverted, but we have a right of privacy. (Even today, many
see defending our privacy as our only legitimate goal.) The lesbian
DOB, outnumbered in a mostly male movement, wanted their
several city chapters separately represented. *ONE* loyalists then
claimed to have previously unmentioned chapters in four cities.

In NACHO, most Easterners aimed to bar groups which they
felt might tarnish our image, and to enforce a common strategy,
emphasizing court appeals, for all homophile groups. They refused
to admit prominent hetero friends to our conferences, and barred
metaphysically-or-sex-oriented groups lest they hurt our image.
It was proposed that groups receive representation proportion-
ate to their membership, but the Credentials committee couldn't
validate membership claims, so each certified group got five votes,
whether it had one member or 1,000. Kameny insisted that small,
dedicated groups were more effective anyhow. NACHO sunk in
the endless struggle on credentials.

Every hot-shot leader in NACHO tried to steam-roller the six
successive conferences to legislate the entire movement into doing
things his or her way. Easterners wanted every participant group
to be bound by any resolution the conclave passed. Eastern leaders
demanded focus on litigation to end discrimination. "I don't give
a damn if people don't like me," Dr. Kameny shouted, "so long as
they can't discriminate against me." Most westerners were plural-
ists and emphasized education, community-building, and building Gay political clout. One narrowly passed resolution canceled
another, until, in 1970, Gay Liberation crazies recruited by Morris
Kight and others from the streets trashed and destroyed NACHO.

The debates between NACHO's East and West blocs paled in comparison with the post-Stonewall, hippie-counter culture–New Left radicalism. Here was *real* diversity!

Patrons, led by bartender Lee Glaze, had responded to an August '68 raid at Wilmington, CA's Patch II bar, by pelting police at the station with flowers. Three new-type groups, Metropolitan Community Church, SPREE and HELP resulted. MCC, founded by recently excommunicated Pentecostal minister Troy Perry, was presented as a church open to Gays (they didn't dare say Gay church). Perry catered to his parishioners' mixed denominational backgrounds, and took a lead in new militancy. Few leaders then were as skilled as he at building Gay pride and community feeling. MCC's growth from the first 12 who showed up in Troy's Huntington Park apartment was phenomenal. Even Gay skeptics and heteros found it inspiring. But the prime goals of MCC, to get Gays to heaven or to improve our conditions on earth, came in for years of debate. Cleaning out the sexism and racism from traditional religious liturgy were later and more difficult goals.

HELP was for ten years a sort of legal insurance club mostly for the leather crowd, with added social and legislative goals. It tried to establish a Los Angles Tavern Guild and to improve legal service delivery to Gays.

We started SPREE to honor filmmaker Pat Rocco, who'd given us our first glimpse of Gay romantic films. For ten years as a film, theater and social club, SPREE was well represented in most Los Angeles Gay demonstrations. Though often operating at the giggly-Gay level, we worked to encourage others to make Gay films and plays, providing a warm social climate for (mostly older) sentimental Gay men and a few women.

San Diego priest Pat Nidorf organized DIGNITY for Catholic Gays in early '69. It got rolling in Los Angeles and spread, with hierarchy support in some cities. It worked to heal Gays damaged by clerical homophobia, and to alter the church's anti-Gay stance, making much progress among theologians and priests' and nuns' associations before the shocking 1986 letter from Nazi-trained Cardinal Ratzinger, exiling open Gays from church support.

Dignity however had made a generation of Gay Catholics strong enough to stand up against that.

THE GAY LIBERATION PHASE

Soon after the June, '69 police raid on New York's Stonewall Inn, where customers angrily fought back, precipitating a weekend of revolt, the Gay Liberation Front started our movement's wildest transformation, previewed by San Francisco's Vanguard and its Committee for Homosexual Freedom and by Minneapolis's FREE. Where we had mostly focused on middle class values, new liberationists had vastly different mindsets—different goals and tactics.

The respectability drive gave way to wild self-indulgence. From suit-and-tie, we went to every costume extreme. From asking authorities to define us more nicely, we said we'd define ourselves—and the rest of society as well. Our movement burst out of the three coastal cities that had largely dominated it. In the months after Stonewall, groups started in Billings, MT, Gainesville, FL and Lawrence, KS. The "zap" was invented, a strategy of invading straight offices and meetings to angrily confront homophobes.

Meetings were often exercises in anarchy. Where *Roberts Rules of Order* had intimidated those unskilled at using them, now any call for orderly procedures was labeled elitist. A few Blacks began making demands, often getting pained silence even from Gay Civil Rights movement veterans—though virtually all GLF's took radical positions in support of minority rights. Some new activists hoped to use Gay lib to advance other causes, such as sectarian left parties—and some socio-political conservatives joined GLF but would have been more at home in the older groups.

There was a flurry of experimentation with new social forms, rejecting the theory of monogamy, rejecting private property, building rural and urban communes, hoping their new life styles would alter all of society. Many Gay liberationists intended the total restructuring of society, thinking that if we all dropped out, the Establishment would topple and we could live in freedom. Our conferences often passed resolutions banning the military-industrial complex, the educational system, profit-making business, the churches and monogamy. Those institutions failed to lie down obediently and die.

New issues came forward which seemed essential to some, quite bothersome to others: sexism, racism, ageism, "looksism"; but sexism the most. Part of this wasn't new (racism surely wasn't) but its ramifications and its jargonizing were. Radical Lesbians and male Effeminists announced that oppression of women is the basis of all oppression; homophobia is merely an aspect of that; liberation for men requires surrendering male privilege, and supporting whatever radical women say they want. Being male became a cardinal sin. Many men resisted the idea that sexism is rooted in language, battling over words that had long been in usage. Can we retain the organic integrity of our language and still remove the biases built into it?

RECOGNIZING OUR DIVERSITY

The post-Stonewall era made it more essential to recognize that our differences were *more than mere personality clashes*, or temporary *impediments to be brushed aside*. The often-clashing goals of Lesbians and Gay men became intense, separating us for a while. Still, many Gays, male or female, just wanted society to let us alone; just wanted to have a good time or find that perfect lover; wanted to be just-like-our-neighbors; to feel that our hope lies in putting on a good front, a polished image; to feel that if people only knew how many of us there are in important places, our troubles would go away—this last gambit did *not* work for German Jews.

A few talked about taking arms against the establishment—ignoring the fact that the other side has the heavy artillery; and some wanted to destroy all old Gay groups and businesses.

There are vast strategic differences (and many fail to distinguish between goals and the strategies we use to achieve them): there are those who are convinced we must get non-Gays to front for us, while a few Gays play power brokers. This strategy is regularly subverted by the fact that so many influential Gays stay deep in the closet. Some would throw all our problems on Jesus. Happily few Gay religious leaders are so naive. Others are convinced that a Marxist revolution would end all our oppression—but China, Cuba—and Russia and Eastern Europe until 1989—threw doubt on that. Some see Gay liberation as solely a sexual freedom issue, as in John Rechy's angry novel *Sexual Outlaw*. A few feminists in the era of the "Political Lesbian" began to regard almost all sexuality as a form of male rape.

Many felt sure that if we all dropped out, smoked pot, chanted OM and joined the New Left or Counter Culture (which were never quite the same thing), the so-called Establishment would collapse quickly and our troubles would end. Many hope to build a rainbow coalition of minorities—always half negated by rampant respectabilism [sic] and prejudice in our own and other minorities. Most of these conflicting goals have at least partial validity, but none of their partisans will give up their views easily, if at all. Certainly, short-term goals are easier to agree on—and the larger the city, the more pronounced the conflicts on goals and tactics are. We unite to picket an outstanding homophobe, or to push a specific piece of legislation, but the unity seldom outlasts a week.

Finally, there are those special interests, minorities within our minority: boy lovers, Lesbian separatists, drags, leather and kinky sex groups, transsexuals, ethnic groups, tearoom cruisers, punks, dopers—some of whom scandalize or scare many mainline Gays and Lesbians. Some of these often get excluded from our parades or centers, but if we exclude them today, we discard large parts of our history and of our integrity. We become guilty of the same discrimination we have so long suffered. At any rate, the goals of these special groups introduces even more angry diversity into the mix. Not all of us defend the right to have whip-and-chain parties, or to have sex with minors or in the bushes, especially unsafe sex. Not all of us agree on abortion, though I think most Gay men support women's right to self-determination.

The joyous parades and other events held in many cities each June drew us together and sharpened our differences at the same time. Some wanted celebrations of freedom or diversity, others angry protests, public relations shows or Mardi-Gras-like parties. Many wanted drag queens kept out of the parades, ignoring the drags who kicked things off at Stonewall and the charity fund-raising that drag-ball groups have done for years. Some objected to right or left wing political slogans, or to religious or anti-religious groups—or to AIDS protests "spoiling the fun."

By 1971, Gay service centers were operating in several cities, and a year later, we organized the first heavily staffed multi-service agency in Los Angeles, which, despite most of its founders' apocalyptic anti-establishment ideas, was soon funded by several levels of government. Much radical energy in the movement was felt by some to be drained from confronting the powers-that-be, to providing consciousness-raising, jobs, housing, substance-abuse guidance, counseling for prisoners, the handicapped, transsexuals, seniors and youth. Radical staffers in 1975 nearly destroyed L.A.'s Center, feeling that the "Band-Aid approach" was draining off revolutionary energy.

Gays were starting softball and bowling leagues, ski clubs, choirs and professional caucuses and women's music was beginning to bloom. Gay and feminist bookstores (separate from "adult" stores) began in many cities, also Gay and women's publishing companies, Gay theaters, special interest caucuses, hiking and running clubs, choruses and bands. Gay publications diversified, some becoming very fancy by earlier standards. Many complained that the movement had sold out to consumerism.

THE CHIMERA OF UNITY

In our desperation to escape the bind of ignorance and bias, we often scream out: "Why can't Gays get together?' We blame our disunity on some defect in Gay character. This is naive. Wishing doesn't make it so—it more often leads to sideswipes at those who disagree with what others of us take for granted.

Anita Bryant's 1977 Miami attack on us (calling a Dade County Human Rights ordinance a threat to the nation's children) was a thunderbolt. Self-important Gay power brokers converged on Dade County to run the campaign, driving out everyone whose strategy differed. They had their way, and the defeat was tidal. They blamed everyone but themselves. When Anita promised to take her campaign on the road, allied with anti-feminist Phyllis Schlafly, the shock half emptied the nation's middle-class closets.

Towns too small to have had a gay group before staged outsize anti-Anita rallies. It was as big a turning point as Stonewall. Human Rights Coalitions cropped up in many cities, and became arenas for every sort of Gay extremist and power-grabber. We ripped each other apart.

In crises, we can often come up with a patchwork unity for fighting homophobic attacks or dealing with AIDS. Yet we rarely see eye-to-eye, and California's 1978 Briggs campaign showed surprising virtue in that. Because attempts failed to organize one big committee in each part of the state to carry out the "best" strategy, we won an election we'd probably otherwise have lost.

While the biggies raised the most money, paid one another lavish salaries and bought a few expensive TV spots, Gay radicals reached labor unions and ethnic minorities. Gay Catholics and other religious groups reached local hierarchy, which promised benevolent neutrality, a gain over other cities. By our usual practice, all would have been organized from Los Angeles and San Francisco, with most of the state overlooked. Instead, anti-Briggs groups started in many virgin areas. Each group reached its own constituency, swinging many voters which a unified committee would have ignored. The prime virtue of our diversity is that it gives us a chance to build bridges to *every* sector of the vastly diversified non-Gay community we come from. The Briggs fight taught us that, but the lesson was forgotten in later campaigns, which we lost.

Ex-stockbroker turned hippie, Harvey Milk, had come to San Francisco and run for office three times, building a half wacky, grass roots organization, and bucking the Gay establishment led by

Jim Foster and *Advocate* publisher David Goodstein. In 1978 Milk was elected Supervisor and became a national symbol. After he'd worked against the Briggs initiative, and called for a national Gay March on Washington, Milk and pro-Gay Mayor George Moscone were assassinated by ex-Supervisor and ex-cop Dan White.

The White verdict set off a large Gay riot outside San Francisco city hall. The massive 1979 March on Washington was partly a memorial for Harvey, but many older leaders had opposed that march, and efforts to follow it with a grass roots National Organization of Lesbians and Gays bogged down over the same credentials questions that had buried NACHO.

New national organizations emphasizing professionalism side-stepped the question of being representative, avoiding extreme disagreements by setting up self-perpetuating boards which undertook to speak for the entire Gay community in lobbying and public relations. They aim to do for us what they feel needs to be done, and the rest of us just have to send in our bucks.

In 1979, Harry Hay, Don Kilhefner, Mitch Walker and others launched the Radical Faerie movement (actually, it was already a few years old), exploring the spiritual dimensions of being Gay. Faerie gatherings, in rustic settings, became excited exercises in new consciousness, a mix of guerrilla theater, Hindu mysticism, mud baths and splendiferous costumed dancing in the moonlight, making magic to restore childhood fantasies and the mystic brotherhood of tribal shaman, in an anti-masculine context. Could we recapture our primitive birthright and make it meaningful, or vital, for today's world? The diverse women's spirituality movement was far ahead of them, though both male and female seekers after spirituality were at times quite weird.

To Gay activists shaped by the sixties, it seems that our community has abandoned the fight and sold out for establishment norms, for buttering up elected officials, for rampant consumerism and respectability, for using the movement as a pool in which those on the make can fish for big salaries. Perhaps. But being on the winning team is often a temporary thing. Recent setbacks in the Democratic Party, where we had seemed to have it made, are a hint of that.

The rise of AIDS after 1981, agonizingly killing thousands of our brothers and some sisters, radically altered the styles and goals of our movement. Some felt that it made all other issues irrelevant, at least for the duration.

Wishful thinking aside, there is almost no single course that will get all Gays and Lesbians marching in unison *for long*—though the '87 and '93 marches on Washington were incredible highs—for almost a week each. Even on AIDS, some refuse to believe that sex contact has any part in spreading the disease, or that we should limit our sexual behavior in order to slow the plague. A few still think the whole AIDS crisis is, "a media hype." And AIDS organizations differ on whether to focus on lambasting inadequate government response and pharmaceutical prices, on research, or on helping people with AIDS. They do focus on raising astronomical funds and paying extravagant salaries to executives. I think we need closer examination of alternate cause and treatment theories—even if only to lay them to rest. With our lives at stake, we *must* ask the unaskable questions. Many Lesbians feel, understandably, that too little attention is paid to health problems that kill women.

And there's intense disagreement as to whether the tactics of ACT-UP groups help or hurt our overall cause—though ACT-UP's "bad manners" have undeniably gotten results. Here especially, we need to discuss our disagreements, to try to iron them out.

I don't think politics is our natural game, and I'd gladly let the heteros have it all back—*except* as a minority, we always *stand on the brink of holocaust*. Many Gays think that, except for AIDS, we've already won the brass ring, and never have to fight anymore. Not true. While Gay rights ordinances have passed in many unexpected places, while an increasing number of Gays and Lesbians have won public office in many areas, while we've helped elect many friendly officials, many victories still elude us, and none of our victories are written in stone. Any or all of our gains could be erased overnight. So we always will have to do the political thing, if only to protect our tails. I'd *rather* see us devoting full time to exploring our spirits and building our community—but we must play the straight world's game also.

FINDING OUR COMMON CORE

We needn't leave this discussion with the assertion of our total diversity. We MUST give diversity proper attention, but after doing so, we can hope to understand better the things that draw us together, the threads of commonality in our experience and to bridge some of our differences. Commonality is not the same thing as homogeneity or unity. It won't press us all into one mold, or into the same political campaign, or get us to agree on which are the right tactical moves for today. It won't erase all our disagreements, or the anger that goes with them. But it should draw us into one river, even if it has diverse streams and eddies.

Many think we have only our sexuality in common. Others say we are tied together only by the persecution we suffer. I suspect we are hung up on these ideas because of how our own society defines the difference. Our commonalties lie deeper, but I can't define them. I can only give suggestions.

Growing up often with a feeling of being outsiders is an important element. Gays aren't the only outsiders in this society, but our estrangement goes deep and starts very early, often in our own family. From infancy on we struggle with social expectations about gender. This sets up in each of us *various* lines of accommodation, resistance, resentment or rebellion, shaping our characters by how much we resist, go along with, or deny. Our first goal was self-understanding, trying to figure out why and exactly how we differed from what our parents, peers and teachers expected, seeking others of our kind, and trying to understand what we shared with them.

This gives us some potential advantages, though many Gays fail to develop that potential: an ability for empathy with others; an ability for non-linear thinking; a tendency to relate to others on an "I-Thou" basis, rather than treating others as objects; and an ability to see around corners erected by the straight world; to bridge all the differences in the world.

The first time I was Gay-baited in print, I was called "the man with the grasshopper mind," because I didn't stick to "A-leads-to-B-leads-to-C" thinking. I finally gave up apologizing for not having a straight mind, locked into the belief that everything has a beginning, turning point, and an end, that every effect has a single cause. I like to think we have a potential for holistic thinking, though our hetero education tries to beat it out of us.

Like Near Eastern Gnostics just before and after Christ, who believed that some people were born with a unique Spark which was a tiny fragment from the God of Light, who'd been shattered in a war with the god of this material world, and who worked to reunite each of its scattered Sparks into a Great Light, I feel that Gay love tends toward expansiveness, inclusiveness, and that our Gay love can eventually bind us together, and bridge all the diversities in our own community and in the whole world.

RECAP

Those who feel in their gut that we all want the same thing won't be satisfied. They'll still say we all want only to be able to live without prejudice, oppression or undue restriction.

Let me recapitulate:

Some feel that society will accept us if we behave like straights, if we convince them that we are just like them. Some want only to organize to fight discrimination or to win gay political clout.

Others feel we must educate the public about the varieties of affectional expression or sexual practice, so that prejudice will vanish and we'll be free to behave as our natures dictate. This group seeks more freedom than the first would care for. Some seek the right to have any kind of sex at any time or place with as many partners as we wish.

Others, like Harry Hay, feel we must earn social acceptance and respect by convincing society that we provide needed services which heteros can't provide. I don't feel we can permit ourselves to be dependent *solely* on the goodwill of non-Gays. Radical Faeries aim to cast off hetero conformity, and reawaken the shamanistic spirits that they feel are central to our nature; to revive the talents of witches and such, so we can heal the wounds of hetero society.

Other Gays and feminists believe our society is founded on oppression, and cannot help but oppress us until society itself is turned upside down. Restructuring goals differ endlessly, some seeking only a more peaceful and equitable society, others seeking to end capitalism, religion, racism, inequality, monogamy, gender roles and much else that distinguishes our society now.

Others feel we can't be free unless we get right with God. For some, that involves giving up our sexuality—or at least giving up non-monogamous sex.

Some of you may dismiss most of these differences of opinion as nonsense, but the differences won't go away easily, if at all. If we hope to work on *some* things together, we must try to understand these radically differing goals, *and* be aware that each goal dictates a unique line of strategies and tactics. So don't be surprised the next time another Gay or Lesbian starts saying or doing something which you are convinced will defeat "our goal." Take our diversity as a rich treasure and try to find ways to work with it. It ain't easy.

Lord, it sure ain't easy!

Eric Rofes

The Emerging Sex Panic Targeting Gay Men
(San Diego, November 16, 1997)

Eric Rofes [1954–2006] was an American educator, author, and activist best known for his extensive efforts working for gay rights and social justice. In the following speech, which he delivered at the National Gay and Lesbian Task Force's Creating Change Conference in San Diego, Rofes discusses the factors at play in American culture that lead to what he calls a "sex panic" specifically targeted at homosexual men.

HISTORIAN ALLAN Berube has defined a "sex panic" as a "moral crusade that leads to crackdowns on sexual outsiders." It is distinct from ongoing harassment and vilification of the sexual fringe. It requires the following components: ideology, the machinery and the power to transform ideology into action, and scapegoated populations, sites, and sexual practices.

During a sex panic, a wide array of free-floating cultural fears are mapped onto specific populations who are then ostracized, victimized, and punished. As Gayle Rubin has observed, historically we have seen that when moral panics are over, countless individuals and groups have suffered greatly and the original triggering social problems have not been remedied.

Gay men have no corner on the market on sex panics. In recent years, we have seen sexual terrors marshaled to create a stampede mentality to trample upon many groups including prostitutes and other sex workers, African-American men, welfare mothers, sex offenders as a class, and men who engage in consensual sex with male teenagers.

Are We Confronting a Sex Panic Today?

Currently debate rages among sectors of gay male communities about whether contemporary spates of police entrapments, closures of commercial sex establishments, encroachments on public sex areas, and vilification of specific gay male subcultures constitute a sex panic. It is important to distinguish between ongoing waves of harassment and victimization and a full-scale sex panic because, while both are destructive of lives and communities, a sex panic alone is characterized by a sustained period of intensified persecution of sexual minorities involving punitive state action, public disgrace, and a powerful cultural dynamic of scapegoating, shaming, and silencing of alternative viewpoints. While communists were harassed and persecuted in this nation during the 1940s, it took the coalescing of a variety of cultural factors in the late 1940s and early 1950s to create the moral panic we have come to know as "The McCarthy Period."

I believe we may be witnessing the early stages of an emerging sex panic focused on sexually-active gay men who do not organize their sex and relationships following heteronormative models. It is at different stages in different locations. For example, I believe this sex panic has emerged in New York City with a sustained, intensified period of policing, harassment, and closure of many gay sex spaces and an accompanying discourse in the media about the need to halt continuing gay male HIV infections. In places like Los Angeles, Miami, Washington, D.C., Austin, and Providence, it is clearly at an earlier stage. Sex panic looks different in urban, small city, and rural areas and will have different characteristics, contexts, and trajectories.

What we are witnessing in 1997 are several powerful social shifts which could easily and swiftly fall into place, causing a full-scale sex panic to break out nationwide at any time. This is the way terror and scapegoating operate in a postmodern culture. At least four factors are contributing to a mounting sex panic:

1. The ascendancy and entrenchment of the Far Right and their development, testing, and successful utilization of sex as a wedge issue which speedily divides liberals and Leftists, their primary opponents.

2. The redistribution and intense concentration of wealth creating vast economic disparities and making the urban centers of our nation sites of contentious class-based battles over massive corporate land-grabs.

3. A shift in public awareness from the belief that gay men had stopped transmitting HIV to the realization that gay men continue to become infected with HIV at significant levels. This is accompanied by many gay men and lesbians' feelings of embarrassment, shame, and outrage.

4. The relative success of gay rights efforts where certain victories are offered predicated on the sacrifice of certain sectors of our communities or the squelching of certain social, cultural, or sexual processes which seem different from heterosexual social norms.

Why Are the Current Debates Flaring Into Sexual Civil Wars?

The emerging sex panic appears to be shaping up as characterized by an ideology which believes gay men's sex is not only sinful and predatory, but is responsible for an escalating AIDS epidemic. We are seeing the machinery and the power to transform ideology into action emerging in media frenzies over gay men's sex, the conceptualization of current health problems as public health emergencies, the use of exceptional measures to restrict sex spaces by public officials, and extreme actions by police officers and other representatives of state power to curtail the sexual activity and drug use of gay men. Media accounts are increasingly scapegoating specific populations—at this moment, circuit boys are the scapegoat-of-choice—sites such as bathhouses, sex clubs, and circuit parties, and activities such as "barebacking." It is also characterized by the active involvement and, in some cases, instigation and leadership of gay and lesbian journalists, political leaders, public officials, HIV prevention workers, and other public health officials.

This is precisely what makes the current debates problematic and why many have such powerful feelings of rage and betrayal:

- 20 years ago we heard Anita Bryant and Paul Cameron insisting gay male sex is diseased and suicidal and these days we hear gay men saying the exact same thing.
- 20 years ago we fought heterosexuals in the mainstream media who invaded our sex spaces and wrote lurid, uninformed accounts of our sex cultures. These days it's gay men working in the mainstream media who invade the spaces and write the same lurid stories.
- 20 years ago it was heterosexual public officials who ordered crackdowns on gay bars, mass entrapment at rest stops, and the intense regulation, policing, and closure of sex clubs. These days it could be queer public officials ordering such actions.

Those of us defending gay male sex cultures are not indifferent to HIV prevention efforts. Many of us are leaders in both areas. We know that effective prevention is build on sexual empowerment and believe that decades of public health research show that tactics of guilt, fear, and repression exacerbate public health crises rather than deter them. It is precisely because many people have become frustrated with HIV prevention and feel at a loss to chart new directions for our work, that the time is ripe for an escalation of support for coercive measures to stop gay men's sex.

Those of us standing up for sexual freedom are neither lost in a romanticized version of the golden age of the 1970s nor dick-hungry men who are selfishly seeking more power and more privilege. We have been condescendingly characterized as immature children who haven't grown up and need to get with the times, put our pricks back in our pants, and apply our energies to the real challenges facing our communities, like gays-in-the-military or gay marriage. Yet we believe that even a cursory look at the histories of our movement will show that sexual liberation has been inextricably bound together with gay liberation, the women's movement, and the emancipation of youth. Among the most effective ways of oppressing a people is through the colonization of their bodies, the stigmatizing of their desires, and the repression of their erotic energies. We believe continuing work on sexual liberation is crucial to social justice efforts.

Those of us taking action to monitor, de-track, and resist the emerging sex panic find ourselves increasingly at odds with mainstream gay efforts to present a sanitized vision of our people which has replaced butch/femme dykes with Heather and her two mommies and kinky gay men with domestic partner wedding cakes. Can we not advocate for a pluralistic queer culture where we affirm everyone's right to self-determination in the ways they organize their sexual relations and construct their kinship patterns?

How Can We Prevent a Full Scale Moral Panic Over Gay Men's Sex?

People who want to stave off the emerging moral panic should go home and organize local activist groups like queers of all genders have done in New York and San Francisco. I hope you write letters and hold the media and public officials accountable for their actions and refuse to renounce our movement's historic linkage with sexual liberation. And I encourage you to continue our efforts at HIV prevention but refuse to support a panic-based response to continuing gay male seroconversions or feel that current infections diminish our communities' contributions to the fight against AIDS of the past 15 years.

For those of you who are ambivalent about such organizing, and for mainstream gay groups who are scared to touch these issues with a ten foot pole, let me say one thing: When full moral panics flare history has shown, in Lillian Hellman's words, it's "scoundrel time" and there are limited roles from which social actors can choose. There are the scoundrels who blow the whistle, point the finger, name the names. There are the resistors who take the risk, go out on the limb, take the fall, and get trampled in the mindless, outraged stampede. And there are the vast masses who find themselves locked in silence by confusion, misgivings, self-protection, ambivalence, and fear. When the panic is over and attention has shifted to other issues, when we all shake our heads and say "How did we ever let it get to that stage?" these people are complicit in the destruction. There is no neutral here.

Please consider three final points.

1. Regardless of your confusion or misgivings stand up firmly against any efforts which mobilize arms of the state to restrict the right of sexual and reproductive self-determination. You don't like sex clubs, don't go to sex clubs. But do not ask your local authorities to shut them down. You don't like sex areas in parks, don't go to sex areas in parks, but don't invite police to bust the men who enjoy such activities.

2. Refuse to cast off any section of our community in order to gain privileges and social acceptance. Demand a continuing commitment to a pluralistic vision of community. Resist scapegoating subcultures you don't know and you don't understand.

3. Try to understand the historic role sex cultures have played in the formation of queer identities and communities and resist seeing them simply as an unfortunate by-product of antigay oppression. Are our sex cultures evidence of our stigmatization, abuse, and reprobation? Or, to borrow James Baldwin's language about a parallel matter, can they be understood as "cultural patterns coming into existence by means of brutal necessity" and can they be seen as strategies for survival?

Perhaps the real trouble with gay men's sex cultures, in a time when many in our communities are replicating heterosexual patterns of social organization, is that they alone give testimony to the fact that gay men as a class have not completely assimilated.

Elizabeth Toledo

Life, Liberty, and the Pursuit of Happiness:
The GLBT Movement at a Crossroads
(Washington, D.C., April 25, 2000)

Elizabeth Toledo has been a national leader for feminist causes since the early 1990s, serving as the Vice President of Action for the National Organization of Women, the Vice President of Communications for Planned Parenthood Federation of America, and the Executive Director of the National Gay and Lesbian Task Force. The following speech was given at the National Press Club.

GOOD MORNING. I am here this morning to discuss the state of the gay, lesbian, bisexual and transgender movement for equality in the United States.

As many state legislatures across the land wrap up their work and adjourn, we are seeing a frenzied pace of legislative activity surrounding GLBT issues. For only the second year in our movement's history, we have seen bills favorable to our community outnumber unfavorable bills—and the ratio is rapidly increasing. So far this year, the National Gay and Lesbian Task Force has tracked 466 bills, of which 288 are favorable and 178 are unfavorable. By comparison, last year, we tracked 269 favorable bills and 205 unfavorable bills.

A trend has emerged which shows that although the gay, lesbian, bisexual and transgender population remains under fierce attack, the movement toward civil rights for all is steadily gaining strength.

Today the Vermont House of Representatives is poised to give final approval to a bill that would allow same-sex couples the right to enter into official civil unions sanctioned by the state. If approved and signed into law, the Vermont bill will do what no state has ever done before—it will provide same-sex couples with all of the rights, benefits and responsibilities of marriage that a state can offer.

Vermont has garnered a lot of attention, and rightfully so. But did you know about Georgia? Indiana? Maine? Alabama? Georgia this year for the first time ever has passed and enacted a hate crimes law. Indiana has passed and enacted a hate crimes data collection law. While not a full-blown hate crimes law, it represents the first time Indiana legislators have ever reacted favorably to a GLBT issue. Maine has passed and forwarded to the voters a full-scale civil rights law that includes sexual orientation. In Alabama, the House has passed an historic bill adding sexual orientation to the existing hate crimes law. The bill is scheduled to come up for a hearing in the Senate tomorrow.

Five states—Mississippi, Nebraska, New Hampshire, New Mexico, Wisconsin—have defeated attempts to either pass or strengthen anti-same-sex marriage laws.

The pace of activity this year continues a trend we first noticed in 1999, a breakthrough year for the GLBT movement. Last year's legislative victories included historic advances in such disparate states as California, Kentucky, New Hampshire and Nevada. In California, legislators passed and the governor signed a trio of bills that established a statewide registry for same-sex couples, added sexual orientation to the nondiscrimination clauses under the state Fair Employment and Housing Act and offered public school students some protection against discrimination on the basis of sexual orientation.

In Kentucky, two cities and two counties adopted pro-GLBT civil rights measures. In New Hampshire, a law preventing same-sex couples from adopting children was repealed. And Nevada became the 11th state to ban job discrimination on the basis of sexual orientation.

While we have largely picked up in the year 2000 where we left off, the news is not all good. Two states—Utah and Mississippi— have passed bills preventing same-sex couples from adopting children. Two state legislatures—Colorado and West Virginia—passed laws preventing same-sex couples from marrying, and California voters approved a measure banning the state from recognizing same-sex marriages in other states. The number of states that have explicitly passed laws banning same-sex marriage will reach 33 if the Colorado governor signs that state's legislation.

Such activity reflects the unfortunate reality of our movement. There is a checkerboard quality to the legal and cultural victories for the LGBT movement, and too often the difference between legitimacy and illegitimacy in the eyes of society may rest on something as arbitrary as a state boundary. Many residents of this country assume that the great strides of the civil rights movement have afforded broad protection against discrimination for all. In fact the legal reality is that those of us in same sex relationships have not been fully protected from discrimination in housing, jobs, family law, education—virtually every aspect of our lives is subject to discrimination and sadly, hate violence or harassment remains a reality in every state in the nation.

Too often the cultural strides that are made in the media, in places of worship, in schools and universities and in the workplace are misinterpreted as a sign that equality has been won.

I'll give you an example. The National Gay and Lesbian Task Force frequently receives phone calls from same-sex couples asking for a list of states in which they can legally marry. These individuals see shows like "Will and Grace" or "Dawson's Creek." They worship in churches or synagogues that welcome them. They are out in the workplace or at school. They just assume, like many heterosexual Americans, that the barriers of discrimination have been eradicated.

The reality, of course, is quite different. Not a single state allows same-sex marriage. Thirty-nine states allow gay, lesbian, bisexual and transgender employees to be fired from our jobs. Twenty-eight states lack hate crimes laws that include sexual orientation. Eighteen states criminalize loving, same-sex relationships.

Today the GLBT movement is at a crossroads. We are under open assault by those who would deny us basic human rights, and at the same time the nation is witnessing a surge in support for our cause. Our lives, our liberty, our pursuit of happiness depend upon our ability to build strong political infrastructure and organize on the state and local level.

Local organizing has always been the trademark of the National Gay and Lesbian Task Force. Fortunately, we are not alone. Today, the state and local political infrastructure of the GLBT movement in the United States is stronger than it has ever been before.

In 1996, NGLTF helped found the Federation of Statewide LGBT Political Organizations. This federation consists of political groups that fight for equality. In just four years' time, the Federation has grown to represent members in every state in the union, an incredible rate of growth in such a short period of time.

With the Federation's help, last year NGLTF was able to produce the largest grassroots mobilization in our movement's history. We helped organize some 350 rallies and other events in all 50 state capitals, plus D.C. and Puerto Rico, during a one-week period. Our campaign—called "Equality Begins at Home"—and the work of the Federation paved the way for the wonderful successes we have seen in the past year.

Now many state legislatures are wrapping up their business and adjourning. Attention will soon shift to the November election—and what could be the most important election of our generation. The GLBT voting bloc has proven to be one of the most powerful constituencies in the country in recent election cycles. If our voters are motivated to go to the polls and elect supportive leaders, we could have the opportunity to shape groundbreaking legal protection. If the nation elects leaders who are hostile to all that NGLTF stands for, we could witness a serious backlash to our hard-won gains.

Dr. Martin Luther King once said the moral arc of the universe is long but bends toward justice. Dr. King was right—but with our continued organizing and mobilization, we can make that moral arc bend much more quickly.

Elizabeth Birch

First Convention Speech by a Gay Organization's Leader
(Democratic National Convention, August 15, 2000)

*Elizabeth Birch [born 1956] is an American attorney and gay rights
activist best known for her work as the Executive Director of the Human
Rights Campaign, an organization dedicated to working for Lesbian,
Gay, Bisexual, and Transgender equal rights. This speech was the
first ever given at a national political convention by the leader of a gay
organization.*

I AM honored to speak here as a gay American. Tonight, we celebrate the American family. But we know that America's family
is not yet whole.

For the color of his skin, James Byrd Jr. was dragged behind a
truck in Jasper, Texas, until his body was shattered on a drainage
ditch. Because of her faith, 14-year-old Kristi Beckel was gunned
down as she worshipped in a Texas Baptist church.

Because Matthew Shepard was gay, he was driven into the
countryside on a freezing Wyoming night, beaten and hung on a
fence to die. His gentle voice still asks why, as do the families who
have paid for our national lesson with their children's lives.

Tonight, we dedicate ourselves to healing the fractures—
soothing the wounds—to making our American family truly
whole. It is now well settled that Democrats are capable of strong

and disciplined standards of governance for our economy, domestic and foreign affairs. But true leadership also requires a muscled heart for equality.

Wise leadership never takes refuge in silence.

I speak here tonight with the parents and political leaders whose action or apathy will determine the fullness of the American family. To parents—some of whom have left their gay children at the margins of family life and out of a vision for America, I say this: I want you to know that your gay children are gifted and strong. All are heroic in the way they have conquered barriers to their own self-respect. Many have suffered cruelty or violence. Some serve their communities with leadership and grace. Many are rich in faith, and have a deep love for this nation and democracy. Tens of thousands have served with distinction in the armed forces. Many have lost their lives.

Until this administration, many battled AIDS virtually alone in the face of a stony, silent government. Many have lost their jobs. All were created by God. And you have a right to be proud of each and every one of them.

I am proud to know the good heart of Al Gore. He has led this nation with wisdom and courage. His vision embraces every child and every family, including my family. I cannot imagine a better leader for our small twins than the next President of the United States, Al Gore.

The other party's vision for America excludes as many as it includes. To be blunt, the Republican platform remains shameful. Healing America's family requires resolve, not simply a refrain.

I do not believe that the Republican ticket is comprised of hateful men. But they are not wise men. They practice silent apathy in the face of hatred, and call it leadership. They forego invective but embrace indifference, and call it compassion.

Deep within their hearts, they know this to be true: that not a single gay American seeks special rights or favored treatment. We seek simple equality—the equal right to work, raise a family, serve our country in every way and be free from the shackles of brutality and hate.

Equality is a special right—a right so special that for two-and-a-quarter centuries it has motivated men and women to dream and to die and to animate the heart of America itself.

Al Gore and Joe Lieberman have taken strong, courageous, positions on behalf of equality. The Democratic platform they support is a work of art in democracy—unambiguously supporting inclusion for every American. They have never run for cover of silence.

Like most Americans, they understand that:

As long as a young man can be left on a fence to die, our American family is fractured;

As long as gay parents live in fear that their children might be taken from them, our family is torn;

As long as hardworking Americans can be fired in 30 states simply for being gay, our family is not whole;

As long as gay people are barred from serving openly and with dignity in the armed forces of the United States, our family is not just;

As long as gay, lesbian, bisexual and transgender youth are at risk for suicide;

Until there is a cure for AIDS for men, women and children here and around the world . . . then the American family we celebrate tonight is not yet healed. It is not enough to love your own child. Leaders must love all children and safeguard the family called America. This is what Al Gore knows. It is what George Bush has yet to learn. We don't have a single child to spare—and we don't have time for George Bush to learn on the job.

I do not know how our young twins will one day judge my partner Hilary and me as parents, or as people. Our hope and prayer is that we will measure up in the way Dr. Martin Luther King asked people to judge themselves. He said: "In the end, we will remember not the words of our enemies, but the silence of our friends."

Let us not follow the silence of George Bush. Let us follow a voice of courage and wisdom, and let us elect Al Gore President of the United States.

Evan Wolfson

Marriage Equality and Lessons for the
Scary Work of Winning
(September 30, 2004)

Evan Wolfson [born 1957] is an American attorney, civil rights activist,
and the founder of Freedom to Marry, a national organization that advo-
cates for the legalization of same-sex marriage. The following speech was
given at the National Lesbian and Gay Law Association's "Lavender
Law" conference.

America in a Civil Rights Moment

One of the good things about my job is I have plenty of time on
planes and trains in which to read.

Right now I'm reading the Library of America's anthology,
Reporting Civil Rights. In two volumes, they've collected the jour-
nalism of the 1940's, '50s, '60s, and '70s, describing the blow-by-
blow, the day-to-day, of what the struggles of those years felt and
looked like . . . before those living through that moment knew
how it was going to turn out.

Exhilarating, empowering, appalling, and scary.

That's what a civil rights moment feels like when you are living
through it—when it is uncertain and not yet wrapped in mythol-
ogy or triumphant inevitabalism [sic].

This year our nation celebrated the 50th anniversary of *Brown v. Board of Education*.

But what followed *Brown* was not the sincere and insincere embrace it gets today, but—in the words of the time—

- legislators in a swath of states declaring "massive resistance"
- billboards saying "Impeach Earl Warren," the then-Chief Justice who wrote the decision
- members of Congress signing resolutions denouncing "activist judges" (sound familiar?)
- and, of course, the marches, Freedom Rides, organizing summers, engagement, hard work, violence, legislation, transformations . . . pretty much everything we today think of as the civil rights movement—all *after Brown*.

America is again in a civil rights moment, as same-sex couples, their loved ones, and non-gay allies struggle to end discrimination in marriage. A robust debate and numberless conversations are helping our nation (in Lincoln's words) "think anew" about how we are treating a group of families and fellow citizens among us. Today it is gay people, same-sex couples, LGBT individuals and their loved ones and non-gay allies—we—who are contesting second-class citizenship, fighting for our loved ones and our country, seeking inclusion and equality—and it is scary as well as thrilling to see the changes and feel the movement.

How can we get through this moment of peril and secure the promise?

There are lessons we can learn from those who went before us . . . for we are not the first to have to fight for equality and inclusion. In fact, we are not the first to have to challenge discrimination even in *marriage*.

The Human Rights Battlefield of Marriage

You see, marriage has always been a human rights battleground on which our nation has grappled with larger questions about what kind of country we are going to be—

- questions about the proper boundary between the individual and the government;
- questions about the equality of men and women;
- questions about the separation of church and state;
- questions about who gets to make important personal choices of life, liberty, and the pursuit of happiness.

As a nation, we have made changes in the institution of marriage, and fought over these questions of whether America is committed to both equality and freedom—in at least four major struggles in the past few decades:

- We ended the rules whereby the government, not couples, decided whether they should remain together when their marriages had failed or become abusive.

  Divorce transformed the so-called "traditional" definition of marriage from a union based on compulsion to what most of us think of marriage today—a union based on love, commitment, and the choice to be together and care for one another.
- We ended race restrictions on who could marry whom, based on the traditional "definition" of marriage, defended as part of God's plan, seemingly an intractable part of the social order of how things have to be.
- We ended the interference of the government in important personal decisions such as whether or not to procreate, whether or not to have sex without risking a pregnancy, whether or not to use contraceptives—even within marriage.
- And we ended the legal subordination of women in marriage—thereby transforming the institution of marriage from a union based on domination and dynastic arrangement to what most of us think of it as today—a committed partnership of equals.

Yes, our nation has struggled with important questions on the human rights battlefield of marriage, and we are met on that battlefield once again.

Patchwork

As in any period of civil rights struggle, transformation will not come overnight. Rather, the classic American pattern of civil rights history is that our nation goes through a period of what I call in my book, *Why Marriage Matters*, "patchwork."

During such patchwork periods, we see some states move toward equality faster, while others resist and even regress, stampeded by pressure groups and pandering politicians into adding additional layers of discrimination before—eventually—buyer's remorse sets in and a national resolution comes.

So here we are in this civil rights patchwork. On the one hand, as the recent powerful and articulate rulings by courts in Washington and New York states demonstrated in the past few weeks, several states *are* advancing toward marriage equality, soon to join Massachusetts in ending discrimination and showing non-gay Americans the reality of families helped and no one hurt.

Meanwhile, on the other hand, as many as a dozen states targeted by opponents of equality as part of their own ideological campaign and for their political purposes could enact further *discriminatory* measures this year, compounding the second-class citizenship gay Americans already endure.

These opponents—anti-marriage-equality, yes, but also, anti-gay, anti-women's equality, anti-civil-rights, anti-choice, and anti-separation-of-church-and-state—are throwing everything they have into this attack campaign because they know that if fair-minded people had a chance to hear the stories of real families and think it through, they would move toward fairness, as young people already have in their overwhelming support for marriage equality.

Most important, as Americans—

- see the faces and hear the voices of couples in San Francisco,
- witness the families helped and no one hurt in Massachusetts and digest the reassuring way in which marriage equality is already finding acceptance there after just a few months,

- engage in conversations in every state and many families, chats with people like us and non-gay allies
- hearts and minds are opening and people are getting ready to accept, if not necessarily yet fully support, an end to discrimination in marriage.

The Union a House Divided

In past chapters of civil rights history unfolding on the battlefield of marriage, this conversation and this patchwork of legal and political struggles would have proceeded in the first instance—and over quite some time—in the *states*, without federal interference or immediate national resolution.

That's because historically, domestic relations, including legal marriage, have under the American system of federalism been understood as principally (and almost entirely) the domain of the states.

States worked out their discrepancies in who could marry whom under the general legal principles of comity, reflecting the value of national unity. The common-sense reality that it makes more sense to honor marriages than to destabilize them was embodied in the relevant specific legal principle, generally followed in all states—indeed, almost all jurisdictions around the world—that a marriage valid where celebrated will be respected elsewhere, even in places that would not themselves have performed that marriage.

States got to this logical result not primarily through legal compulsion, but through common sense—addressing the needs of the families and institutions (banks, businesses, employers, schools, etc.) before them. Eventually a national resolution came, grounded, again, in common sense, actual lived-experience, and the nation's commitment to equality, constitutional guarantees, and expanding the circle of those included in the American dream.

But when it comes to constitutional principles such as equal protection—and, it now appears, even basic American safeguards such as checks-and-balances, the courts, and even federalism—anti-gay forces believe there should be a "gay exception" to the constitution, to fairness, and to respect for families. Inserting the federal government into marriage for the first time in U.S. history, *our opponents* federalized the question of marriage, prompting the passage of the so-called "Defense of Marriage Act" (DOMA) in 1996.

This federal anti-marriage law creates an un-American caste system of first and second class marriages. If the federal government likes whom you marry, you get a vast array of legal and economic protections and recognition—ranging from Social Security and access to health care, to veterans benefits and immigration rights, to taxation and inheritance, and a myriad of others (in a 2004 report the GAO identified 1,138 ways in which marriage implicates federal law). Under so-called DOMA, if the federal government doesn't like whom you married, this typically automatic federal recognition and protection are withdrawn in all circumstances, no matter what the need.

The federal anti-marriage law also purported to authorize states not to honor the lawful marriages from other states (provided those marriages were of same-sex couples)—in defiance of more than two hundred years of history in which, as I said, the states had largely worked out discrepancies in marriage laws among themselves under principles of comity and common sense, as well as the constitutional commitment to full faith and credit.

When this radical law was first proposed, some of us spoke up immediately saying it was unconstitutional—a violation of equal protection, the fundamental right to marry, federalist guarantees such as the full faith and credit clause, and limits on Congress's power. Ignoring our objections, our opponents pressed forward with their election-year attack.

Now they concede the unconstitutionality of the law they stampeded through just eight years ago, and are seeking an even more radical means of assuring gay people's second-class citizenship, this time through an assault on the U.S. Constitution itself, as well as the constitutions of the states.

Because they do not trust the next generation, because they know they have no good arguments, no good reason for the harsh exclusion of same-sex couples from marriage, our opponents are desperate to tie the hands of all future generations, and as many states as possible, now.

This patchwork—and especially the next few weeks and months—will be difficult, painful, even ugly, and we will take hits. Indeed, we stand to take several hits in the states where our opponents have thrown anti-gay measures at us in their effort to deprive our fellow-citizens of the information, the stories of gay couples to dispel stereotypes and refute right-wing lies, and the lived-experience of the reality of marriage equality. While it is especially outrageous that the opponents of equality are using constitutions as the vehicles for this division and wave of attacks on American families, in the longer arc, their discrimination will not stand.

Here are a few basic lessons we can cling to in the difficult moments ahead, to help us keep our eye on the prize of the freedom to marry and full equality nationwide, a prize that shimmers within reach.

Lesson #1—Wins Trump Losses

While we stand to lose several battles this year (2004), we must remember that wins trump losses.

Wins trump losses because each state that ends marriage discrimination gives fair-minded Americans the opportunity to see and absorb the reality of families helped and no one hurt when the exclusion of same-sex couples from marriage ends. Nothing is more transformative, nothing moves the middle more, than making it real, making it personal—and seeing other states join Canada and Massachusetts will be the engine of our victory.

Lesson #2—Losing Forward

Even where we cannot win a given battle, we can still engage and fight so as to at least lose forward, putting us in a better place for the inevitable next battle.

Now let me say a little more about this idea of "losing forward."

After all, as someone most famous for the cases I lost, I've built an entire career on it.

Losing forward is a way that all of us can be part of this national campaign, no matter what our state. Even the more challenged states, the states with the greater uphill climb, the states where we are most outgunned and under attack—even those of us in the so-called "red states" still have a pivotal part in this national movement and can make a vital contribution.

In *every* state—even those where we cannot win the present battle, but fight so as to lose forward—we have the opportunity to enlist more support, build more coalitions, and make it possible for more candidates and non-gay opinion-leaders to move toward fairness. All this contributes to the creation of the national climate of receptivity in which some states may cross the finish line before others, but everyone can be better positioned to catch the wave that will come back to every state in this national campaign.

Work on the ground in Georgia, for example, can get us a Bob Barr speaking out against the constitutional amendment, or make districts safe for African-American leaders or "surprising" voices to speak out in support of marriage equality. Work in Michigan— while perhaps not enough to win this round—can still help enlist prominent labor or corporate leaders to our cause.

And, working together, this national chorus will indeed swell, with some states further along and all participating, until all are free.

Wins trump losses. As long as we repel a federal constitutional amendment and continue to see some states move toward equality, beating back as many attacks as possible and enlisting more diverse voices in this conversation, we will win.

Lesson #3—Tell the Truths

Now, the principal reason we are going to take hits this year and lose many, if not all of the state attacks in November is because our opponents are cherry-picking their best targets and depriving the reachable middle of the chance to be reached. They have more of a head start, more money and more infrastructure through their mega-churches and right-wing partners . . . and fear mongering at a time of anxiety is easy to do. And, of course, historically, it is difficult to win civil rights *votes* at the early stage of a struggle.

But, to be honest, there is another reason, too, that we will not do well in most of these votes this year. Quite simply, our engagement, our campaigns in almost all of these states—are "too little, too late." We are starting too late to have enough time to sway people to fairness . . . and we are giving them too little to think about to guide them there. We have to avoid that error in the next wave of battles we face next year, which means, from California to Minnesota, from Wisconsin to Maine, starting not too late, but now, and by saying the word truly on people's minds, doing it right.

Put another way, the country right now is divided roughly in thirds. One-third supports equality for gay people, including the freedom to marry. Another third is not just adamantly against marriage for same-sex couples, but, indeed, opposes gay people and homosexuality, period. This group is against any measure of protection or recognition for lesbians and gay men, whether it be marriage or anything else.

And then there is the "middle" third—the reachable-but-not-yet-reached middle. These Americans are genuinely wrestling with this civil rights question and have divided impulses and feelings to sort through. How they frame the question for themselves brings them to different outcomes; their thinking is evolving as they grapple with the need for change to end discrimination in America.

What moves that middle?

To appeal to the better angels of their nature, we owe it to these friends, neighbors, and fellow citizens to help them understand the question of marriage equality through two truths:

Truth 1—Ending marriage discrimination is, first and foremost, about couples in love who have made a personal commitment to each other, who are doing the hard work of marriage in their lives, caring for one another and their kids, if any. (Think couples like Del Martin and Phyllis Lyon who've been together more than fifty years.) Now these people, having in truth made a personal commitment to each other, want and deserve a legal commitment.

Once the discussion has a human story, face, and voice, fair-minded people are ready to see through a second frame:

Truth 2—The exclusion of same-sex couples from marriage is discrimination; it is wrong, it is unfair, to deny these couples and families marriage and its important tangible and intangible protections and responsibilities. America has had to make changes before to end discrimination and unfair treatment, and government should not be denying any American equality under the law.

When we see lopsided margins in these votes, it means that under the gun in the first wave of electoral attacks, we have not as yet reached this middle. We can't be surprised *not* to win when in so many campaigns, and over so many opportunities to date (electoral campaigns and just month-to-month conversations), we have failed to give this middle third what they need to come out right.

When, in the name of "practicality" or advice from pollsters or political operatives, we fail to put forward compelling stories and explain the realities of what marriage equality does and does not mean, it costs us the one chance we have to do the heavy-lifting that moves people. *We wind up not just not winning, but not even losing forward.*

By contrast, consider how we lost forward in California.

In 2000, we took a hit, when the right wing pushed the so-called Knight Initiative and forced an early vote on marriage. We lost the vote, but because there had been some, though not enough, education about our families and the wrongs and costs of discrimination, polls showed that support for marriage equality actually rose after the election. And the very next year, activists pressed the legislature to enact a partnership law far broader than had been on the table in California before then. Our engagement over marriage continued, and within a couple years, legislators voted again, this time in support of an "all but marriage" bill, which takes effect this coming January. And California organizations and the national legal groups continue to engage for what we fully deserve—pursuing litigation in the California courts and legislation that would end marriage discrimination.

If we do our work right, making room for luck, we may see marriage in California, our largest state, as soon as next year.

To go from a defeat in 2000 to partnership and all-but-marriage in 2004 with the possibility of marriage itself in 2005—that's called *winning*.

Lesson #4—Generational Momentum

Remember, we have a secret weapon: death.

Or to put it more positively, we on the side of justice have generational momentum. Younger people overwhelmingly support ending this discrimination.

Americans are seeing more and more families like the Cheneys, and realizing, with increasing comfort, that we are part of the American family. The power of the marriage debate moves the center toward us, and as young people come into ascendancy, even the voting will change.

This is our opponents' last-ditch chance to pile up as many barricades as possible, but, again, as long as we build that critical mass for equality and move the middle, we win.

The Stakes

Why is it so important that we *now* all redouble our outreach, our voices, our conversations in the vocabulary of marriage equality?

- In part, because victory is within reach.
- In part, because we can and must move that middle now to make room for that generational momentum and rise to fairness.

- In part, because America is listening and allies are increasing.
- In part, because this is our moment of greatest peril.
- And, in part, because the stakes are so great.

What is at stake in this civil rights and human rights moment?

If this struggle for same-sex couples' freedom to marry were "just" about gay people, it would be important—for gay men and lesbians, like bisexuals, transgendered people, and our non-gay brothers and sisters—are human beings, who share the aspirations for love, companionship, participation, equality, mutual caring and responsibility, protections for loved ones, and choice.

Yes, if this struggle were "just" about gay people, it would be important, but it is not "just" about gay people. If this struggle were "just" about marriage, it would be important, for marriage is the gateway to a vast and otherwise largely inaccessible array of tangible and intangible protections and responsibilities, the vocabulary in which non-gay people talk about love, clarity, security, respect, family, intimacy, dedication, self-sacrifice, and equality. And the debate over marriage is the engine of other advances and the *inescapable* context in which we will be addressing all LGBT needs, the *inescapable* context in which we will be claiming our birthright of equality and enlarging possibilities for ourselves and others.

Yes, if this struggle were "just" about marriage, it would be important, but it is not "just" about marriage.

What is at stake in this struggle is what kind of country we are going to be.

- Is America indeed to be a nation where we *all*, minorities as well as majorities, popular as well as unpopular, get to make important choices in our lives, not the government, or a land of liberty and justice only for some?
- Is America indeed to be a nation that respects the separation of church and state, where government does not take sides on religious differences, but rather respects religious freedom while assuring equality under the law, or a land governed by one religious ideology imposed on all?

- Is America to be a nation where two women who build a life together, maybe raise kids or tend to elderly parents, pay taxes, contribute to the community, care for one another, and even fight over who takes out the garbage are free and equal, or a land where they can be told by their government that they are somehow lesser or incomplete or not whole because they do not have a man in their lives?

All of us, gay and non-gay, who share the visions of America as a nation that believes that all people have the right to be both different and equal, and that without real and sufficient justification, government may not compel people to give up their difference in order to be treated equally—all of us committed to holding America to that promise have a stake in this civil rights/human rights struggle for the freedom to marry.

And if we see every state, every methodology, every battle, every victory, and even every defeat as part of a campaign—and if we continue to enlist non-gay allies and voices in this campaign, transforming it into a truly organic *movement* for equality in the grand American tradition,

- we will move the middle,
- we will lose forward where necessary,
- we will empower the supportive,
- and we will win!

We *are* winning.

There is no marriage without engagement.

Let's vote in November, get others to vote in November, and move forward in our work to win, working together, doing it right.

Paul Martin

The Civil Marriage Act
(February 16, 2005)

*Paul Edgar Phillipe Martin [born 1938] is a Canadian politician who
served as the twenty-first Prime Minister of Canada (2003–2006). Martin gave the following speech in support of the Civil Marriage Act at the
Canadian House of Commons (Bill C-38).*

I RISE today in support of Bill C-38, the Civil Marriage Act. I rise
in support of a Canada in which liberties are safeguarded, rights
are protected and the people of this land are treated as equals
under the law.

This is an important day. The attention of our nation is focused
on this chamber, in which John Diefenbaker introduced the Bill of
Rights, in which Pierre Trudeau fought to establish the Charter of
Rights and Freedoms. Our deliberations will be not merely about
a piece of legislation or sections of legal text—more deeply, they
will be about the kind of nation we are today, and the nation we
want to be.

This bill protects minority rights. This bill affirms the Charter
guarantee of religious freedom. It is that straightforward, Mr.
Speaker, and it is that important.

And that is why I stand today before members here and before
the people of this country to say: I believe in, and I will fight for,

the Charter of Rights. I believe in, and I will fight for, a Canada that respects the foresight and vision of those who created and entrenched the Charter. I believe in, and I will fight for, a future in which generations of Canadians to come, Canadians born here and abroad, will have the opportunity to value the Charter as we do today—as an essential pillar of our democratic freedoms.

There have been a number of arguments put forward by those who do not support this bill. It's important and respectful to examine them and to assess them.

First, some have claimed that, once this bill becomes law, religious freedoms will be less than fully protected. This is demonstrably untrue. As it pertains to marriage, the government's legislation affirms the Charter guarantee: that religious officials are free to perform such ceremonies in accordance with the beliefs of their faith.

In this, we are guided by the ruling of the Supreme Court of Canada, which makes clear that in no church, no synagogue, no mosque, no temple—in no religious house will those who disagree with same-sex unions be compelled to perform them. Period. That is why this legislation is about civil marriage, not religious marriage.

Moreover—and this is crucially important—the Supreme Court has declared unanimously, and I quote: "The guarantee of religious freedom in section 2(a) of the Charter is broad enough to protect religious officials from being compelled by the state to perform civil or religious same-sex marriages that are contrary to their religious beliefs."

The facts are plain: Religious leaders who preside over marriage ceremonies must and will be guided by what they believe. If they do not wish to celebrate marriages for same-sex couples, that is their right. The Supreme Court says so. And the Charter says so.

One final observation on this aspect of the issue: Religious leaders have strong views both for and against this legislation. They should express them. Certainly, many of us in this House, myself included, have a strong faith, and we value that faith and its influence on the decisions we make. But all of us have been elected to serve here as Parliamentarians. And as public legislators, we are responsible for serving all Canadians and protecting the rights of all Canadians.

We will be influenced by our faith but we also have an obligation to take the widest perspective—to recognize that one of the great strengths of Canada is its respect for the rights of each and every individual, to understand that we must not shrink from the need to reaffirm the rights and responsibilities of Canadians in an evolving society.

The second argument ventured by opponents of the bill is that government ought to hold a national referendum on this issue. I reject this—not out of a disregard for the view of the people, but because it offends the very purpose of the Charter.

The Charter was enshrined to ensure that the rights of minorities are not subjected, are never subjected, to the will of the majority. The rights of Canadians who belong to a minority group must always be protected by virtue of their status as citizens, regardless of their numbers. These rights must never be left vulnerable to the impulses of the majority.

We embrace freedom and equality in theory, Mr. Speaker. We must also embrace them in fact.

Third, some have counseled the government to extend to gays and lesbians the right to "civil union." This would give same-sex couples many of the rights of a wedded couple, but their relationships would not legally be considered marriage. In other words, they would be equal, but not quite as equal as the rest of Canadians.

Mr. Speaker, the courts have clearly and consistently ruled that this option would offend the equality provisions of the Charter. For instance, the British Columbia Court of Appeal stated that, and I quote: "Marriage is the only road to true equality for same-sex couples. Any other form of recognition of same-sex relationships . . . falls short of true equality."

Put simply, we must always remember that "separate but equal" is not equal. What's more, those who call for the establishment of civil unions fail to understand that the Government of Canada does not have the constitutional jurisdiction to do so. Only the provinces have that. Only the provinces could define such a regime—and they could define it in 10 different ways, and some jurisdictions might not bother to define it at all. There would be uncertainty. There would be confusion. There would certainly not be equality.

Fourth, some are urging the government to respond to the decisions of the courts by getting out of the marriage business altogether. That would mean no more civil weddings for any couples.

It is worth noting that this idea was rejected by the major religions themselves when their representatives appeared before the Standing Committee on Justice and Human Rights in 2003. Moreover, it would be an extreme and counterproductive response for the government to deny civil marriage to opposite-sex couples simply so it can keep it from same-sex couples. To do so would simply be to replace one form of discrimination with another.

Finally, Mr. Speaker, there are some who oppose this legislation who would have the government use the notwithstanding clause in the Charter of Rights to override the courts and reinstate the traditional definition of marriage. And really, this is the fundamental issue here.

Understand that in seven provinces and one territory, the lawful union of two people of the same sex in civil marriage is already the law of the land. The debate here today is not about whether to change the definition of marriage—it's been changed. The debate comes down to whether we should override a right that is now in place. The debate comes down to the Charter, the protection of minority rights, and whether the federal government should invoke the notwithstanding clause.

I know that some think we should use the clause. For example, some religious leaders feel this way. I respect their candor in publicly recognizing that because same-sex marriage is already legal in most of the country, the only way—the only way—to again make civil marriage the exclusive domain of opposite-sex couples is to use the notwithstanding clause.

Ultimately Mr. Speaker, there is only one issue before this

House in this debate. For most Canadians, in most parts of our country, same-sex marriage is already the law of the land. Thus, the issue is not whether rights are to be granted. The issue is whether rights that have been granted are to be taken away.

Some are frank and straightforward and say yes. Others have not been so candid. Despite being confronted with clear facts, despite being confronted with the unanimous opinion of 134 legal scholars, experts in their field, intimately familiar with the Constitution, some have chosen to not be forthright with Canadians. They have eschewed the honest approach in favour of the political approach. They have attempted to cajole the public into believing that we can return to the past with a simple snap of the fingers, that we can revert to traditional definition of marriage without consequence and without overriding the Charter. They're insincere. They're disingenuous. And they're wrong.

There is one question that demands an answer—a straight answer—from those who would seek to lead this nation and its people. It is a simple question: Will you use the notwithstanding clause to overturn the definition of civil marriage and deny to Canadians a right guaranteed under the Charter?

This question does not demand rhetoric. It demands clarity. There are only two legitimate answers—yes or no. Not the demagoguery we have heard, not the dodging, the flawed reasoning, the false options. Just yes or no.

Will you take away a right as guaranteed under the Charter? I, for one, will answer that question, Mr. Speaker. I will answer it clearly. I will say no.

The notwithstanding clause is part of the Charter of Rights. But there's a reason that no prime minister has ever used it. For a prime minister to use the powers of his office to explicitly deny rather than affirm a right enshrined under the Charter would serve as a signal to all minorities that no longer can they look to the nation's leader and to the nation's Constitution for protection, for security, for the guarantee of their freedoms. We would risk becoming a country in which the defence of rights is weighed, calculated and debated based on electoral or other considerations.

That would set us back decades as a nation. It would be wrong for the minorities of this country. It would be wrong for Canada.

The Charter is a living document, the heartbeat of our Constitution. It is also a proclamation. It declares that as Canadians, we live under a progressive and inclusive set of fundamental beliefs about the value of the individual. It declares that we all are lessened when any one of us is denied a fundamental right.

We cannot exalt the Charter as a fundamental aspect of our national character and then use the notwithstanding clause to reject the protections that it would extend. Our rights must be eternal, not subject to political whim.

To those who value the Charter yet oppose the protection of rights for same-sex couples, I ask you: If a prime minister and a national government are willing to take away the rights of one group, what is to say they will stop at that? If the Charter is not there today to protect the rights of one minority, then how can we as a nation of minorities ever hope, ever believe, ever trust that it will be there to protect us tomorrow?

My responsibility as Prime Minister, my duty to Canada and to Canadians, is to defend the Charter in its entirety. Not to pick and choose the rights that our laws shall protect and those that are to be ignored. Not to decree those who shall be equal and those who shall not. My duty is to protect the Charter, as some in this House will not.

Let us never forget that one of the reasons that Canada is such a vibrant nation, so diverse, so rich in the many cultures and races of the world, is that immigrants who come here—as was the case with the ancestors of many of us in this chamber—feel free and are free to practice their religion, follow their faith, live as they want to live. No homogenous system of beliefs is imposed on them.

When we as a nation protect minority rights, we are protecting our multicultural nature. We are reinforcing the Canada we value. We are saying, proudly and unflinchingly, that defending rights—not just those that happen to apply to us, not just that everyone approves of, but all fundamental rights—is at the very soul of what it means to be a Canadian.

This is a vital aspect of the values we hold dear and strive to pass on to others in the world who are embattled, who endure tyranny, whose freedoms are curtailed, whose rights are violated.

Why is the Charter so important, Mr. Speaker? We have only to look at our own history. Unfortunately, Canada's story is one in which not everyone's rights were protected under the law. We have not been free from discrimination, bias, unfairness. There have been blatant inequalities.

Remember that it was once thought perfectly acceptable to deny women "personhood" and the right to vote. There was a time, not that long ago, that if you wore a turban, you couldn't serve in the RCMP. The examples are many, but what's important now is that they are part of our past, not our present.

Over time, perspectives changed. We evolved, we grew, and our laws evolved and grew with us. That is as it should be. Our laws must reflect equality not as we understood it a century or even a decade ago, but as we understand it today.

For gays and lesbians, evolving social attitudes have, over the years, prompted a number of important changes in the law. Recall that, until the late 1960s, the state believed it had the right to peek into our bedrooms. Until 1977, homosexuality was still sufficient grounds for deportation. Until 1992, gay people were prohibited from serving in the military. In many parts of the country, gays and lesbians could not designate their partners as beneficiaries under employee medical and dental benefits, insurance policies or private pensions. Until very recently, people were being fired merely for being gay.

Today, we rightly see discrimination based on sexual orientation as arbitrary, inappropriate and unfair. Looking back, we can hardly believe that such rights were ever a matter for debate. It is my hope that we will ultimately see the current debate in a similar light; realizing that nothing has been lost or sacrificed by the majority in extending full rights to the minority.

Without our relentless, inviolable commitment to equality and minority rights, Canada would not be at the forefront in accepting newcomers from all over the world, in making a virtue of our multicultural nature—the complexity of ethnicities and beliefs that make up Canada, that make us proud that we are where our world is going, not where it's been.

Four years ago, I stood in this House and voted to support the traditional definition of marriage. Many of us did. My misgivings about extending the right of civil marriage to same-sex couples were a function of my faith, my perspective on the world around us.

But much has changed since that day. We've heard from courts across the country, including the Supreme Court. We've come to the realization that instituting civil unions—adopting a "separate but equal" approach—would violate the equality provisions of the Charter. We've confirmed that extending the right of civil marriage to gays and lesbians will not in any way infringe on religious freedoms.

And so where does that leave us? It leaves us staring in the face of the Charter of Rights with but a single decision to make: Do we abide by the Charter and protect minority rights, or do we not?

To those who would oppose this bill, I urge you to consider that the core of the issue before us today is whether the rights of all Canadians are to be respected. I believe they must be. Justice demands it. Fairness demands it. The Canada we love demands it.

Mr. Speaker: In the 1960s, the government of Lester Pearson faced opposition as it moved to entrench official bilingualism. But it persevered, and it won the day. Its members believed it was the right thing to do, and it was. In the 1980s, the government of Pierre Trudeau faced opposition as it attempted to repatriate the Constitution and enshrine a Charter of Rights and Freedoms. But it persevered, and it won the day. Its members believed it was the right thing to do, and it was.

There are times, Mr. Speaker, when we as Parliamentarians can feel the gaze of history upon us. They felt it in the days of Pearson. They felt it in the days of Trudeau. And we, the 308 men and women elected to represent one of the most inclusive, just and respectful countries on the face of this earth, feel it today.

There are few nations whose citizens cannot look to Canada and see their own reflection. For generations, men and women and families from the four corners of the globe have made the decision to chose Canada to be their home. Many have come here seeking freedom—of thought, religion and belief. Seeking the freedom simply to be.

The people of Canada have worked hard to build a country that opens its doors to include all, regardless of their differences; a country that respects all, regardless of their differences; a country that demands equality for all, regardless of their differences.

If we do not step forward, then we step back. If we do not protect a right, then we deny it. Mr. Speaker, together as a nation, together as Canadians: Let us step forward.

Ian Hunter

A Matter of Interest
(June 17, 2009)

Ian Hunter is an Australian politician in the Australian Labor Party, best known for becoming the first openly gay member of the South Australian Legislative Council with his election in 2006. In the following speech, delivered in the Legislative Council, Hunter accuses Prime Minister Kevin Rudd of personally preventing him from marrying his partner of twenty years.

I RISE today to speak about a matter close to my heart. I want to get married.

But I can't—I can't marry the person I love; not in my own country at least.

Prime Minister Kevin Rudd says he and his government believe that marriage should be maintained as the union between a man and a woman. If that's his opinion—fair enough. Everyone is entitled to their opinion. But to impose his personal beliefs on the rest of the community is just wrong.

Going on from that, the Prime Minister has added that the government might look at partnership registrations some time in the future.

Well, I might have accepted that—20 years ago. But times and the issue has moved on. Registration is no longer good enough.

I no longer think that it is adequate that I might one day be able to go to the local council and register my partnership as I might register my dog. I want to get married.

Around the world, the fight for marriage equality has been going on—and around the world, states, courts, community and parliaments have been rising to the fight. They are deciding that homosexual and heterosexual couples can choose to marry, and can be treated exactly the same way.

The Netherlands, Belgium, Canada, South Africa, Norway, Sweden and Spain have all legalised same-sex marriage, as have the U.S. states of Massachusetts, Connecticut, Iowa, Maine and Vermont. It looks like New York is pretty close, too, and of course there is the on-going debate in California.

Add to that the list of countries where civil unions are recognized—from the United Kingdom to Luxembourg, and many in between—and you start to realize how completely out-of-step Australia is beginning to look with those nations that we like to compare ourselves with. What a sad state of affairs when the nation that pats itself on the back for being the country of a "fair go for all" denies its citizens this very basic right.

Now, it might be that I am out of step with many of you here in this Chamber—and I might even be out of step with some in my party—and I'm certainly out of step with Prime Minister Rudd on this issue—but I stand here today to let him and everyone else know that second best is no longer an option.

I am no longer content to accept the crumbs from the table.

I am no longer willing to accept a reinforced second-class status.

I am no longer prepared to accept a proposition that my married friends' relationships are intrinsically superior to my relationship.

And I certainly won't accept the proposal that means my relationship is registered at the local council or some similar body.

Because partnership registration is about *death*—and what happens to your estate on your death. Marriage is about *life*—how you live your life publicly in a loving relationship with a partner and with our *families*.

I want to get married. Next year will be the twentieth anniversary of my not-being-married to my partner, Leith. Yes, I could travel to Massachusetts or South Africa and get married there. But that is not my preferred option: I want to share my marriage with my family and my friends—like we all do.

No one has ever been able to provide me with an adequate response as to why marriage should be confined to a man and a woman. The response that this form of "traditional marriage" should be retained because of the biblical tradition doesn't hold much water for all of us who have no interest in getting married in a church—and last year, that was more than 60 percent of all couples who exchanged vows.

The ability to bear and raise children is another reason often given for standing against gay marriage. You know what? I know plenty of gay parents who are wonderful parents; and I know plenty of straight couples who don't have children, either through choice or circumstance. So that doesn't hold up either as an argument.

As for the sanctity of marriage being threatened by gay marriage—all I can say to that is: if your heterosexual marriage is going to be somehow devalued by your homosexual neighbours' marriage, that says more about your relationship than it does about mine.

The marriage equality debate is gathering speed around the world and yet Australia finds itself once again a backwater in this debate. It is time for the community's voice to be raised, calling for marriage equality and I add my voice to that call today.

Because I want to get married—and you, Mr. Rudd, are stopping me.